UNTAPPED LEADERSHIP

HARNESSING THE POWER OF UNDERREPRESENTED LEADERS

Jenny Vazquez-Newsum

 Prometheus Books

Essex, Connecticut

Prometheus Books

An imprint of Globe Pequot, the trade division of
The Rowman & Littlefield Publishing Group, Inc.
4501 Forbes Blvd., Ste. 200
Lanham, MD 20706
www.rowman.com

Distributed by NATIONAL BOOK NETWORK

British Library Cataloguing in Publication Information Available

Library of Congress Cataloging-in-Publication Data Available

ISBN 978-1-63388-916-3 (paper) | ISBN 978-1-63388-917-0 (ebook)

∞™ The paper used in this publication meets the minimum requirements of American National Standard for Information Sciences—Permanence of Paper for Printed Library Materials, ANSI/NISO Z39.48-1992.

For Chase and Maeve

CONTENTS

PART III: LEADERSHIP LESSONS FROM AN ESSENTIAL STANDPOINT

AUTHOR'S NOTE

Thank you for being here with this book. I look forward to your reactions and reflections on the concepts posed.

Before we begin, I have a quick note on language. As the book's title indicates, we explore the power and contributions of historically underrepresented leaders. You'll quickly notice that, in the text, I use the term "marginalized" predominantly. Although the leaders included in this book may also be considered underrepresented in leadership, underrepresentation is the symptom rather than a cause. Marginalization is often at the root of that underrepresentation and therefore felt like the more accurate term when discussing leadership. To approach this discussion head-on, I am challenging us to build comfort in naming things clearly and with more specificity, even if it is tougher to say or to hear.

The text also uses terms like *BIPOC* and *leaders of color* interchangeably, and I acknowledge the challenges with this terminology. An accidental erasure occurs when we condense Black, Indigenous, Latinx/a/o, Asian, South Asian, and Middle East and North Africa experiences together. The groups within these racial identities are not monolithic but lumping them together under one term inadvertently suggests otherwise. For the purpose of this book, however, I am speaking about a collective that emerges specifically through racial marginalization in leadership. As a result, I've used these terms to support readability and clarity throughout the text.

There is much more work that can and should be done to explore the specific leadership contributions of distinct groups. Although racial diversity is at the core of this book, underrepresented leadership also exists among those who are marginalized because of their sexual orientation, gender identity, physical abilities, religion, neurodiversity, and other identities. There is also a particular leadership expertise that exists when individuals experience their careers at the intersection of these identities.

As we explore the pages to come, there are aspects of all of us that are marginalized in leadership as a result of how we have come to define and practice it. It is my hope that *Untapped Leadership* is merely the first step in uncovering those overlooked elements, which we can do by following the lead of racially underrepresented leaders.

INTRODUCTION

What to Expect in This Book

When searching for the top leadership books of today, it doesn't take long to notice that white men predominantly write these books: more than 90 percent of the authors are white and male. Words like *war*, *laws*, and *power* stare us down from their covers. They confidently purport that the secrets to leadership exist, often very neatly, within the bounds of their pages, a dominance on leadership development that has run unchecked and unquestioned. Notably, the handful of books written by women edges toward candor, introversion, and vulnerability—these authors seemingly tiptoe into the conversation, suggesting that another way to lead may exist. Finding titles written by BIPOC authors requires considerably more digging.

If we pause to examine the foundations of leadership theory, we should not be surprised that the limited perspectives fueling leadership frameworks are rooted therein. Our ground-floor use of the word *leadership* in the United States begins with the nineteenth-century "great man theory," aptly named by and for those who would benefit tremendously from coining themselves as a "great man." Great man theory relied heavily on the now-debated concept that leaders are born with attributes that set them apart from others. It studied the characteristics of heroes—but of course, only certain ones—which was the perfect setup to exclude women; Black, Indigenous, and other people of color; and anyone else who didn't fit the bill. In so doing, it created the theoretical structure to centralize power within a dominant group.

Although scholarship ultimately rejected great man theory, nearly all proposed leadership frameworks since have originated from white male researchers and executives. Coupling this with the persistent reality that white men are significantly overrepresented in executive positions, it seems great man theory lost steam in name but remains alive and well in practice.

In her TED talk, author Chimamanda Ngozi Adichie talks about the Igbo word *nkali*, which translates to English as "to be greater than another," and its role in how stories communicate power. She explains, "Like our economic and political worlds, stories too are defined by the principle of *nkali*: how they are told, who tells them, when they're told, how many stories are told are really dependent on power."[1]

From the nineteenth century until present day, a select group of storytellers have been shaping and communicating leadership from perspectives that excluded others. Given its membership within the dominant group in our society, it is no coincidence that it emerged as the "authority" on the subject. By commanding the bookshelves and airtime on leadership's story, this group continues to reinforce the foundation that great man theory established two centuries ago, ultimately preserving power for those who hold it. It is a systemically sound design.

This reality elicits the need to explore another approach. What are the other stories of leadership? What do they teach us? How can we expand the picture beyond what has been traditionally authored? Specifically, what strategies do leaders of color employ that reimagine how impactful leadership looks?

When leadership exists in an uneventful cockpit, no one pays much attention to the pilot who lands a plane in perfect weather. What would be celebrated, studied, and considered exemplary is the pilot who successfully lands a plane when the conditions are fraught with difficulties. With this model in mind, *What would it look like to study the leadership of those who lead under challenging conditions?*

When the environment is not ideal?

When decisions are riskier?

When they carry more significant societal burdens as they lead?

What does leadership look like when operating in systems that are not built for your success?

Those we have traditionally deemed as leadership authorities have been flying their planes in clear skies, providing the rest of us with often oversimplified lists and laws on how to make our ascent. Though the advice is well intended, these leaders seem completely unaware that our environmental forecast is much less conducive for flying.

Through the leadership experiences of leaders of color, *Untapped Leadership* explores what other realities exist—the undercurrents, the subtle strategies, and the unmired commitment to lead amid risky environments. Our experiences are not the same as those written about in those leadership books. We cannot access some of those touted behaviors, decision-making models, and approaches and be received in the same manner as the writers of those books. This book examines the unspoken realities of leadership as a person of color—leadership that exists across all levels of organizations, flexing and contorting to survive and thrive. As a result, BIPOC leaders are positioned to be the twenty-first-century leadership so desperately needed.

In Part I: Leadership in Context, I offer a critical examination of the popular leadership frameworks that have underpinned publications and rhetoric on the subject yet systematically have excluded the majority of the population during their creation. In the 1840s, great man theory and trait theory produced the first studies of leadership, basing their analysis on the personal attributes of men with charisma, intelligence, and wisdom. Slavery existed until 1865, effectively omitting Black men and women from consideration. In the 1940s, a shift in research resulted in task-oriented versus people-oriented leadership frameworks. Recall that Jim Crow laws would not end for another twenty-five years, and women's suffrage passed just two decades prior (except for Black women, who were not able to vote until 1965). In the early 2000s, situational leadership theories emerged, indicating that what makes a leader great depends on the situation. Around the same time, the first two Black Fortune 500 CEOs *ever* were hired, with white men holding 96 percent of CEO roles.[2]

Given the contexts within which these frameworks were developed—by homogenous groups studying similarly homogenous leaders—the theoretical picture of leadership is at best incomplete and at worst deeply flawed.

In Part II: The Capacities of Underrepresented Leaders, I fill in the picture with the experiences and expertise of leaders of color. Given their unique standpoint as marginalized leaders navigating within a dominant culture, leaders of color tap into highly skilled and effective strategies yet are undermined and overlooked. To survive and thrive, BIPOC leaders deploy unique approaches that until now have not been studied and named. Throughout *Untapped Voices*, you learn stories about leaders of color sharing their unique perspectives and expertise. What results is an exploration of leadership that challenges our traditional notions of what it looks like and who exercises it.

You'll also find reflection prompts to "tap in" and spark your own ideas about how to reimagine leadership from overlooked perspectives. Change happens in micro-moments, and the "tap in" prompts offer you micro-opportunities for leadership shifts. Each chapter also breaks down specific actions you can take whether you identify as a marginalized leader or not. Given how much is overlooked in traditional definitions of leadership, I hypothesize that some aspect of your leadership is also unrecognized or pushed aside. I offer ways for you to access those underused areas and invite others to do the same.

In the final section, Part III: Leadership Lessons from an Essential Standpoint, I offer frameworks for individuals and organizations to employ that are built on the lessons gained from an increased understanding of the valuable expertise of leaders of color. Until now, our leadership models have not represented the vastness and diversity of other existing approaches, leaving us with a limited and limiting perception of what is possible. Our world exists in a permanent state of crisis needing reimagining and renewal. We need a new way to lead—one that is nuanced, contextual, dynamic, purpose driven, and connected. It is time to listen and learn from the leadership authority of people of color.

As a result of reading this book, you will:

- develop a more critical lens through which to examine the sources of our current leadership rhetoric;
- name and understand the experiences of leaders of color, offering a more comprehensive and realistic understanding of leadership; and
- access expanded leadership strategies for your career, regardless of your identity.

You may see yourself within these pages. Or you may deepen your awareness, realizing you haven't had the complete picture all this time. You may shed some interpretations of leadership that do not serve you. You may adopt new ones that do. Ultimately, we will begin building a new foundation from which to inclusively learn and lead.

PART I

LEADERSHIP IN CONTEXT

> When I saw my leadership questioned, I sought guidance from a couple of leadership books, but none of them resonated.
>
> —Victoria, research and evaluation consultant in higher education, Latinx

1

THE SHAKY FOUNDATION OF LEADERSHIP

A common sight in metropolitan cities are deep excavations in the ground signaling the beginnings of future apartment buildings, skyscrapers, and other real estate projects. Once built, we admire their architecture, engage within the buildings' walls, and navigate around them with little thought to their roots. Yet to sustain what we see, construction teams must meticulously and thoroughly develop a strong, stable foundation below ground that can hold the building's weight. Without this, a building is susceptible to cracking, sinking, or shifting, endangering everything within. Environmental elements can cause subtle erosion that, if unnoticed for too long, deteriorates the building to the point of being uninhabitable. In other words, any structure is only as solid as its foundation.

Similar to the buildings we see, our current definitions and frameworks of leadership began with a foundation; the vocabulary we use to discuss it and our perceptions of what leadership entails all started somewhere. Before we can properly examine current structures—or what we see now—we need to begin with the foundation and what has been built since leadership research and rhetoric began two centuries ago. As we note cracks, weak walls, and sinking corners in the leadership house we have built, understanding what is actually happening requires us to go underground to observe what we have not considered. We need to explore the base, which has informed whose leadership we value in our society, for no matter the distance between where we started and where we are now, the foundation stays the same. That sub-terranean construction and engineering created the parameters within which we have defined what—and *who*—leadership looks and sounds like, so any serious discussion of such things must start here.

As we dig into the foundation of fundamental leadership theories in our history, we begin with the inception of the modern-day use of the word *leadership*, which emerged in the English language in the nineteenth century. In the 1840s, the Scottish writer Thomas Carlyle began writing about the leadership contributions of society's greatest heroes and thus emerged the base of our foundation and the first leadership theory—the great man theory. Carlyle arrived at the great man theory, noting that "the history of the world is but the biography of great men."[1] According to Carlyle, these great men possessed the wisdom and charisma needed to lead. Great man theory goes as far as to suggest that these men also were favored with divine influence, emphasizing that one needed to be born with this favor. As can be imagined, this interpretation was incredibly convenient for those who fit the bill for greatness, offering them a bit of divine untouchability.

Of course, great man theory didn't apply to *all* men, and it definitely did not include women. The men who fit the parameters often had the opportunity to be "great" due to aristocratic benefits connected to their membership within white society. For historical context, when Carlyle's work took hold, slavery in the United States had persisted for centuries, women could not vote, and the poor of any color or gender had minimal influence in society. As we delve into the subsurface levels of current leadership structures, we find that great man theory was designed through and for exclusion. Only some could be considered great, and the guise of divine intervention and inherent traits protected that greatness. Illiterate, poor, and those with disabilities were excluded, even among white men. Great man theory preserved the positions of the elite, assigning benign but potent language to their manufactured and problematic status at the top of societal hierarchies by calling it "leadership." In doing so, those with proximity to those great men—either through connection or by extension based on similar race and gender identity (as long as they did not also hold other undesirable identities)—could benefit from the potential of being considered a leader. They had a chance whereas those enslaved by those great men were tacitly omitted from consideration. Carlyle's foundational work made the embedded hierarchy palpable yet indiscernible; it helped to make it make sense.

It can be tempting to want to dispel the problematic components of great man theory and shove it into a corner of unfortunate yet antiquated ideas from which we have moved on. But *have* we moved on? The leader-as-hero concept is still present in current interpretations of leadership. We look to those in such positions to save others and to save us. We celebrate heroic efforts, pull out shiny pedestals, and place our leader-heroes on top. We are influenced by the charisma of presidential candidates, at times even more than by their policies, and more often than not, these leader-heroes are predominantly white men. Although we may not explicitly deem this as great man theory in practice, its tenets subversively play out right before our eyes. As antiracist activist and author Ibram X. Kendi notes, "the very heartbeat of racism is denial";[2] the heartbeat of great man theory persists through the unnoticed interplay between its theoretical and rhetorical dismissal and its unchecked existence in our elected offices, boardrooms, and C-suites.

Great man theory paved the way for researchers like Francis Galton to study the traits of eminent men and their relatives to prove that leaders were born with hereditary gifts, not made. In *Hereditary Genius*, published in 1869, Galton attempted to scientifically connect lineages of "eminent men," essentially proving that eminence is inherited.[3] A known eugenicist, Galton further cemented this trait approach to defining leadership in the American psyche as his rhetoric continued to bore down on the hypothesis that the genetically predisposed qualities of a certain few connect to greatness. Arguing for the inherent nature of leadership qualities yet ignoring the structural and societal confines that prevented most of the population from living out those qualities was research negligence, an intentional design, or both. This approach also secured the "leader" title for those genetically tied to these eminent men, cultivating a lineage of perceived prominence by virtue of the mere accomplishment of being born.

Eugenics research and approaches have long been discredited as unscientific; however, it is worth contemplating how much of this foundational idea has permeated our subconscious sentiments about leadership. Once a path has been set, imagining what we have never seen or breaking away in a wildly different direction is generally difficult. An apple may fall far from a tree, but it still sprouts from those branches. With great man theory and the subsequent misleading research of Galton and others, we are pinned to a problematic starting point that is rarely acknowledged in present-day leadership dialogue. The answer to this inherited underpinning is not to disregard and minimize it with a veiled denial of its impact but to explicitly name it and critically examine the resulting permeations. Within that examination are opportunities for reimagination and new approaches in which we can more intelligently determine where we need to diverge or expand. That apple originated from its foundational tree, but its seeds can be cultivated in fresh soil with new, more sustainable and more fruitful techniques, which hopefully yields a better crop in the future.

BEHAVIORAL THEORIES

Great man theory and its offshoots maintained its popularity in the United States until the 1940s, when behavioral theories gained popularity. As implied by the name, behavioral theories attributed leadership to one's behaviors rather than inherent traits. One of the most commonly cited behavioral theory studies emerged from the Ohio State University (OSU). University researchers reduced leadership behaviors into two categories, task focused and people focused, ultimately concluding that influential leaders were those who ranked high in both. Present-day OSU officials consider this behavioral theory as having "revolutionized the way leadership is measured, studied and developed."[4]

Yet as this revolutionary research was taking place, the few Black students attending OSU were not allowed to live on campus.[5] If Black people were not allowed to reside on campus, they surely were not considered for a study on leadership, and it can be assumed that others from marginalized communities were similarly excluded. With a commitment to leadership research of a white male-dominant study population, OSU's work falls quite short of a revolution and essentially builds an additional shaky floor atop of the weak foundation established by Carlyle.

This familiar glossing over of exclusionary practices in leadership research has allowed what should have been considered a limited study to flex and broaden itself into seminal work deemed "revolutionary" and spawn a plethora of descendants. Behavioral theories and attending

6

publications have not only proliferated since, but they have also contributed to a dominant narrative that stems from a source not fully representative. Without pinpointing the context within which the work at OSU emerged, we are caught glancing at a seemingly well-designed building with cracks in its load-bearing walls. We are accepting a framework at face value and have built extensively upon it without questioning whether certain behaviors equated with "leadership" are also tied to fitting in within dominant culture or if such behaviors are inhibited in leaders of color given existing hierarchical societal structures.

SITUATIONAL THEORIES

Along with the civil rights movement, the 1960s brought us situational theories of leadership. Moving beyond behavioral predictors, researchers like Fred Fiedler, Paul Hersey, and Ken Blanchard theorized that a leader's success depended on the situation. At first glance, situational theories seem to incorporate more contextual factors that inform leadership, a promising development to connect theory to reality, but we soon find their limitations.

For example, Fiedler's contingency model examined elements such as how much trust and confidence a leader could garner from followers, which correlated to the degree of power and influence the leader has over consequential decisions such as hiring, firing, and salaries.[6] The model also involves a least preferred coworker (LPC) scale, illuminating the ideal situational factors for those low and high on the scale, including assessment choices such as pleasant versus unpleasant and friendly versus unfriendly. With racial discrimination and violence as the societal backdrop, race and other factors would undoubtedly (if tacitly) play an influential role in LPC scale results and in a marginalized leader's ability to garner the trust and confidence of those in a workplace. The methodical exclusion of people of color likely persisted in Fiedler's research: many were fighting for basic civil rights, let alone the chance to exhibit workplace leadership. In learning that situational theories stopped woefully short of describing deeper contextual factors that influenced the nature of those situations, we must now consider the imperceptible ways that work such as Fielder's perpetuated definitions of leadership that solidified a dominant culture's authority.

It is important to note that many of these studies arrived at such leadership models through rigorous research processes governed by academic standards. Thus, it is equally important to question how "rigor" is defined. Because these researchers excluded groups that were not white and male, the extent to which present-day researchers and practitioners lean on behavioral and situational theories as part of the seminal body of work on leadership begs us to question the reliability of that scholarship. Yet the work remains largely untouched in that respect. Some components may have validity, but the overall picture does not capture the full scope of leadership and therefore is flawed.

On the heels of contingency theory came leader-member exchange (LMX) theory in the 1970s. Originally developed by George B. Graen within the situational theory camp, LMX theory describes a leader's relationship with his team members. What's most troubling about the framework is that it proposes (or, interpreted another way, accurately describes) that leaders will filter their staff into in-groups and out-groups based on workplace exchanges within the leader-member relationship. Those in the in-group are looked upon more favorably and, as a result, are trusted more, receive more meaningful work, and undoubtedly are considered for promotion, raises, and continued professional success within the team. Those in the out-group are just that—out. Due to what is described as incompetence, disagreeableness, or loss of trust, those in a leader's out-group rarely receive the same professional considerations as those in the in-group.

LMX theorists do not shy away from stating that in-group team members can benefit from perceived similarities, positive affect, a likeness in interests, values, or attitudes, and the ability to integrate into a leader's preferences.[7] Based on what we know about those in leadership roles in the 1970s, we can guess that similarity and integration into white professional culture was essential to being part of an in-group. In fact, "negative affect" and neuroticism are two of seven characteristics within this model to have a negative impact on LMX relationships with a supervisor. With plenty of research highlighting how we interpret affect differently in white and Black faces, we should question how many team members of color have been placed in an out-group based purely on bias cloaked in the term "negative affect."

Similarly, when interpreting racial contexts, the negative influence of neuroticism in leader-member exchange also warrants deeper analysis.

Neuroticism has been defined as a "trait disposition to experience negative effects, including anger, anxiety, self-consciousness, irritability, emotional instability, and depression" with an increased likelihood of reacting poorly to environmental stress.[8] In professional spaces and in connection to LMX, we must question how much environment contributes to neuroticism, particularly if one is part of an out-group at work and also a person of color. Those external stressors undoubtedly will be exacerbated for those navigating spaces with a thin sense of belonging, especially when those spaces have a significant impact on one's livelihood, finances, and sense of self-worth. For those not facing such experiences, there is less opportunity for that neuroticism to emerge. In considering this, we discover how a cycle is created, reinforced, misdiagnosed, and justified with research such as LMX theory.

Though not its intention, leader-member exchange theory may explain why white male-dominated in-groups continue to dominate the top positions across all industries; however, the research overlooks the glaring societal factors that likely contributed to those results. Consequentially, LMX theory joins a body of research that neutralizes the impact of these phenomena in general human behavior frameworks, thus embedding such concepts more deeply and subtly into our ingrained assumptions about leadership.

THE REEMERGENCE OF TRAIT THEORIES

In more recent decades, trait theories have reemerged, exposing their extended roots in great man theory and the trait theories from the early twentieth century. A flurry of leadership trait models emerged during the early 2000s, the most frequently cited being the work of Stephen J. Zaccaro. Zaccaro's trait-leadership model includes a non-exhaustive list of traits that leaders should have, including characteristics like agreeableness, extraversion, openness, and creativity.[9] The central hypothesis within trait theory is that leaders innately have these traits, which have been "programmed" since birth. Nature not only supersedes nurture in this case, but nurture is not even considered. For leaders of color navigating challenging work environments, the opportunity to showcase some of these traits can be limited. Expressing innate traits such as creativity and extraversion is not as easy in spaces in which you are the only person of color and do not experience a sense of belonging. We can interpret the agreeableness of marginalized leaders, for example, to the extent that they can "grin and bear it" when they experience a microaggression or learn, as statistics show, that a white male colleague earns more than they do. Similarly, often on the receiving end of damaging conscious and unconscious biases, leaders of color may exhibit these traits, yet others do not perceive or acknowledge them. They could possess a great deal of creativity, yet if it does not align with what a professional culture considers creative or if it goes too far against the established grain, then that trait is missed or misinterpreted. We must remain within professional lines when leading, and the leadership identified by trait theories sets the margins of those lines.

For those outside academia or generally uninterested in reviewing complex statistics and complicated literature regarding trait theories, the takeaway is that leaders are born, not made, and you'd better hope you were born with the right traits. The environments within which leaders thrive as well as the external realities that reward or demote certain traits remain unexamined.

THE PROLIFERATION OF MYERS-BRIGGS TYPE INDICATOR

Although trait theories continue to be the most debated body of leadership research, they persist and permeate. A prime example of their extended and indirect reach is the widely adopted Myers-Briggs Type Indicator, or MBTI. MBTI has been utilized by the vast majority of Fortune 500 companies and beyond. MBTI was created as a personality type assessment, aiming to inform one of his or her innate, unchangeable traits across sixteen types. Although academic researchers have claimed that MBTI does not hold up scientifically, companies, academic institutions, and even general internet culture gravitate to the assessment, making it one of the most widely known, particularly in connection to work. Even though one of MBTI's creators, Isabel Briggs Myers, has documented sentiments with eugenic themes, her pseudoscientific assessment has been used to make hiring decisions and to sort people into roles that most align with their results.[10]

I have taken MBTI at a few junctures in my life, both academically and in professional settings. My result has remained consistent as INTJ—introverted, intuitive, thinking, and judging. Admittedly, the outcomes always seemed to resonate for the most part, confirming, in a way, the creators' claim that the indicator assesses innate, immovable elements of ourselves. In my most recent MBTI training at a prior workplace, the MBTI-certified facilitator also emphasized the unchangeable nature of what the results indicate and provided me with a one-page summary about INTJ personalities. The handout included some of the usual language regarding my inherent preferences, but it also included a bullet point near the bottom noting that African Americans are more likely to have this result. With race being a socially constructed classification system, that bullet point ran counter to the trait narrative the work espouses and made me question how much of my lived experiences informed my "innate" traits. Would I be less introverted if I hadn't been the only woman of color in many of my academic classes throughout graduate school, for example? Given that we are recalling lived experiences when responding to an assessment like MBTI, how can we completely disentangle our inherent traits from learned behaviors? If in fact that statement was true and the INTJ type was most common for Black people, then the MBTI interpretation of that result would not include an environmental explanation: Black people's results would have nothing to do with the way they perceive the world but would be due entirely to what they inherited through genetics. It feels like a bit of residue from Briggs Myers's eugenic sentiments.

What is most troublesome about the massive adoption of MBTI as a professional tool is that it proliferated this personality test widely across workplaces, popularizing elements of trait theories in ways that have unchecked and sometimes unnoticed consequences. MBTI and other assessments like it have been used to make hiring decisions and to assess the type of roles or work one can get. The impact could be professionally consequential as labels and boxes are built for people to fit within. If you choose to explore more about MBTI online, you'll surely come across articles claiming what styles are most likely to be CEOs or to make more money (typically one of the extroverted combinations), reinforcing that only certain types of people are inherently built for leadership. If this sounds familiar, it is because we can trace the dawn of personality trait tests back to Francis Galton, the

UNTAPPED VOICES

What I have learned about leadership that I haven't read about or heard from others is that there is more than one way to lead. Leadership comes in different forms. Some of the best leaders are the ones that are grounded in themselves. As a BIPOC-identifying individual, a lesson that I have learned in leadership that I would want to share with my younger self is that you and your experiences and points of view are enough. A lesson that I would want to share with someone who is not BIPOC is . . . to be open to different points of view that you may not be familiar with or know. Research and learn about other points of view.

—Casey, senior finance and operations adviser
in international development, Black

eugenics researcher determined to scientifically prove genetic and divine sources of leadership. Galton is attributed as the first to create these types of assessments. In fact, if we widen our lens to also examine the commonly used professional assessments such as Big 5, Strengthsfinder, and Enneagram, we see that they and their associated theories have all been developed by white men. The questions asked, the labels and descriptions of the results, the intended uses, and the unintended consequences of the assessments have emerged from a singular, dominant perspective. This is not to say that none of the results from these indicators are useful. The misstep has been our inappropriate reliance on the outcomes, consciously and subconsciously, mislabeling them as an ultimate truth when they are just a sliver of reality and of what we are capable of as diverse beings. These assessments have made ubiquitous the tendency to equate certain traits with leadership.

OUR LIMITED UNDERSTANDING OF LEADERSHIP

What is missing in leadership research is the acknowledgment and awareness of the role that social dynamics like race can play in the workplace.

These frameworks have served as the canon in classrooms, management programs, and executive suites, yet they don't provide the complete picture. Without the inclusion of more voices, the story is flawed, narrated from the incomplete perspective of the dominant leadership class, exclusivity that has been embedded since the beginning. Although these leadership perspectives do not need to be dismissed altogether, it is important to note that other perspectives—from people of color, women, and others with marginalized identities—have been discounted through centuries of research, authorship, and dialogue. If we are to truly understand leadership through rigorous scholarship and practice, then those discounted perspectives must be included on equal footing in studies, syllabi, bookshelves, and keynotes. In those perspectives live unnamed and underrecognized leadership strategies for how to lead under glass ceilings and within glass walls designed from those limited frameworks of our leadership history.

A building is only as solid as its foundation. If the foundation is unstable or otherwise faulty, whatever you construct on top of it will be always problematic. The same goes for leadership research. We can dispel and debate specific theories, as we have with the great man theory and trait theory, but the faulty foundation limits how far we can adjust and evolve from this particular base. Our framework conceptualizes leaders as heroes, leadership requiring followers who are either behind or below, and leading capabilities determined by behaviors, traits, and/or situations. Beyond those parameters, not much has been explored or attempted.

We don't need to add on to the incomplete and wobbly structure that past and current leadership frameworks have created—we need to tear down the house, gut the foundation, and reimagine a new structure (or maybe an environmentally friendly green space) in its place. Without doing so, we cannot move beyond what we know and into the realm of what we need. We will never truly understand the nature of our most pervasive and persistent challenges unless we examine the roots of the types of leadership for which we seek solutions.

The moment demands we reframe leadership by answering those initial questions anew. If we embarked on a modern quest to study leadership, what (or whom) would we find? If more perspectives were included in our research, how would they shift, expand, or challenge those popular frameworks? I hypothesize that we would find nuanced definitions of leadership

UNTAPPED VOICES

To me, embodiment of leadership is driven from within and it's very difficult to fake; that's why it's so effective and transcends formalities and it's what makes it difficult to simply assign—it has to be acquired and integrated. In other words, it's not enough to read a book or listen to a podcast about how to lead people, it has to be wired through a lived experience.

I assume what inhibits recognition of such leadership is lack of awareness, its intangible nature (how do you measure the degree of my embodied leadership and compare it with yours?), and I suspect it's much easier to control and direct a conforming type of leadership rather than account for a nuanced, multilayered, eclectic expression of leadership that reflects more accurately our diverse humanity. Now, I love and appreciate clarity of vision, persistence, resilience, and assertiveness (my association with traditional forms of leadership). However, if you believe in the benefits of embracing human diversity, you have to wonder why we limit ourselves by only focusing on a narrow scope of our being, which is how we are at work. The last couple years have blended the line between home and office; I actually prefer to work with a full human being in all the messy glory than with a shell of a human polished for the office.

—Elena, executive, music licensing, Asian

that may complement traditional approaches and some that may conflict with them. We may discover effective leadership practices that move groups and organizations forward in ways we have not considered before. Ultimately, we would have a more robust body of work that better reflects the realities of all leaders today.

What if we built a new foundation of leadership on the heels of the COVID-19 pandemic and racial awakening of 2020? As we have witnessed the buckling of countless systems and the exposure of inequities across society since 2020, we should question what got us to this point; that is, where and to whom we have looked for leadership and what we have missed by using that familiar gaze. The marginalized in our society have borne the brunt of those crumbling systems across health care, education, housing, and employment, so we should first ask ourselves if having those untapped voices creating and managing those systems in the first place would have better prepared us for a sudden and disorienting pandemic. What if we now shifted the spotlight to the overlooked and undercounted perspectives and allow new voices to develop leadership language and frameworks?

If we were to build a new foundation, how would we change our organizations and repurpose our work? How could we inclusively, creatively, and

UNTAPPED VOICES

I believe leadership is modeling behavior that works to actively dismantle oppressive systems, centers the voices of those who are most impacted by systemic oppression, and is anti-patriarchal and anti-capitalist. This includes centering and exploring values of collectivism, power sharing, and collaborative work, avoiding "either/or" thinking, centering the sustainability of people in their work, vulnerability, and transformational relationship building that does not avoid conflict but rather welcomes it as a tool to get deeper. This is too often undervalued or not valued at all as most conventional conceptions of leadership are modeled on white-dominant cultural values and patriarchal value systems.

Leading with a holistic view of people and of oneself and a commitment to building leadership that centers on people of color, Black, and indigenous populations is needed now more than ever.

I believe that I possess a deep-rooted empathy for all persons I engage with and a commitment to fostering a sense of belonging, a commitment to building with people and not at the expense of people, and [the understanding] that this oftentimes means the process is messy, uncomfortable, and takes a lot longer than we are traditionally told is okay. I believe that this approach helps me to build strong relationships built on trust.

—Clara, director of philanthropy, Latinx

impactfully address our most persistent challenges? As we have learned by looking to the past and present, we are limited in how we have discussed leadership and to whom we look when defining those approaches. If we continue as is, those persistent challenges across our societal systems will continue. Having seen how damaging the result can be for all of us, we cannot allow more of the same. We need leadership frameworks that advance awareness of and accountability for the full context of reality and that innovatively respond to the needs of BIPOC and other underrepresented leaders because we are all better off as a result.

It is time for additional perspectives to lead the way, and we learn more about them in the pages to come.

2

LEADERSHIP IN ITS CURRENT STATE

To understand and explain phenomena, realities, and theories, we often look to the natural world. We have devised mathematical structures, identified cause and effect relationships, and discovered symbiotic exchanges that replicate themselves across a variety of interactions, all by observing nature.

One such source of natural insight is the life cycles of trees. Beginning with the tiniest of seeds and growing to a wide range of heights, trees can be relied upon to do a few things. They establish their roots in the soil. They grow toward the sun. And, for the most part, they branch out in some way. Some trees, like those around my neighborhood in Los Angeles, grow long and thin with swaying palms at the very top. Others reach shorter heights but have thick trunks and heavy foliage. Some trees treat us to sweet fruits with seeds, which seek their own growth journey underground. If we are to consider how the theoretical frameworks of centuries past have informed our interpretations of leadership today, we can study how trees establish their structures, develop foliage, and at times bear fruit. Both begin with the smallest of seeds, whether physically, as is the case for trees, or metaphorically through an idea or a theory, as is the case for leadership. Both establish roots that emerge from those seeds—an embedded and persistent web that lies below the surface. Trees take root to thrive through this nutrient-rich network. Leadership frameworks take root through the narratives and fortifying rhetoric they establish. Both have their exposed elements, visible above ground and in our workplaces. And both reproduce. New seeds

UNTAPPED VOICES

Leadership is bound to cultural norms and practices, and as such, it is also bound with unspoken expectations to lead like the dominant culture. It's hard for people to understand other ways of leading—ways that are outside of the majoritized culture/culture in power.

—Sara, senior human relations specialist for
a nonprofit, South Asian and White

emerge and spread to begin the cycle again. What we define and ultimately experience as leadership breeds more of that leadership or, at the very least, informs what we interpret to be valued in leadership.

As we review the roots of leadership research and rhetoric, we find a direct connection to where we are today. To assume we are not connected to those roots is a grave mistake. Our leadership tree originated from a seed planted with eugenically leaning trait theories and cultivated in soil that only enriched the exclusionary outcomes of its visible elements above the surface. Over time, the tree has grown, shifted its appearance through the seasons, delighting us with distracting fruit or fooling us with unreliable cover that blows over at any sign of environmental elements. Ultimately, however evolved and mature the tree becomes, it is still the same tree that began from that particular seed and enriched itself in that soil. A fruit-bearing tree's bounty may separate and fall from its branch but not very far.

If we are to consider our current interpretations of leadership as the fruit borne of that tree, we have not examined its source closely enough before taking a bite. We have not made the connection that what we see now in leadership is directly informed by the discipline's problematic past. We know our historical context, and yet we do not question its impact on our leadership work in the present day. We still see predominantly cis-hetero white men dominating the leadership space. We still see women struggling with what is referred to as "imposter syndrome," which is in reality an arduous effort to succeed in systems that subtly and explicitly state that they do not belong. We witness people of color systematically overlooked for decision-making positions, even when those decisions are being made on behalf of their own communities, as we commonly witness in nonprofit, philanthropy, education, and even athletic sectors.

We often assume that we have evolved beyond the overt exclusion of our past. However, as we examine the current state of leadership today, the accuracy of that assumption becomes hazy. There remains a glaring gap in representation in leadership discourse and top organizational roles. We are informed by this single story, often implicitly. This monopolization in the field permeates far into the micro-levels of organizations big and small. We build upon this incomplete narrative in the workplace at all stages—from candidate recruitment and hiring to promotions and raises. For example, it is well known that hiring managers judge resumes differently based on the names of the candidates: those who are assumed to be candidates of color—purely on the basis of their names—receive increased scrutiny and fewer callbacks than candidates whose names align with the dominant culture's preferred names.[1] Data emerged decades ago on this reality, and even after increased workplace implicit bias training, the reality continues. We also know that Black employees are less likely to be promoted or receive raises to this day. At the current rate, it will take Black workers ninety-five years to achieve parity at higher organizational levels.[2] Yet the narrative that it is due to a pipeline challenge persists. What in fact is happening—in addition to outright oppression, racism, and discrimination in some cases—is an inherent interpretation of who is fit for leadership and success and who is not. We cannot overlook the role that dominant leadership narratives have played in cultivating this reality. Those narratives are at the very roots of our corporate DNA because, unsurprisingly, the fruit has not made its way too far from the tree. It might not have even fallen off the branch.

We are looking to a subset of people to define leadership based on their own experience of the world and of work. As a result, a limited version of leadership expertise is widely accepted. It is *a* truth, but it is not *the* truth. However, we look toward those perspectives as the truth because that is all that is given to us most often. It is what gets published. It is what gets added to course syllabi. It is what gets the microphone on the stage. And yet, it is not actually representative of the majority of us. We haven't really asked ourselves what else can be true in leadership. We currently hold an incomplete picture, and our organizations—our future—need the complete version of the story for more realistic and impactful definitions.

PRESENT-DAY GREAT MAN THEORY

Because we currently associate leadership with power, those who define *leadership* also hold great power; based on their definitions, we assign those leaders great authority, privilege, and influence. Only a select group in our society have had the opportunity to create these definitions, and not coincidentally they are doing so from inherited and unearned positions in the top echelon of our societal hierarchy. By defining leadership, they continue to solidify their power and standing. Although they did not ask for this complicated reality, they are effectively playing the part.

If we permit only certain perspectives to serve as the authority on leadership, then we are implicitly indicating whom we deem fit to lead. To whom we look to define leadership influences who we believe is qualified to lead in our companies, and we continue to watch it play out. As of 2021, women of color account for only 4 percent of C-suite leaders.[3] Among Fortune 500 CEOs in 2021, only 1.2 percent were Black, 4 percent were Latinx, and 8 percent were Asian.[4] Looking beyond the Fortune 500, at the entire economy's chief executives, only 5.9 percent are Black, 6.8 percent are Asian, and 7.2 percent are Latinx.[5] The numbers do not improve when we look at boards—only 21 percent of S&P 500 directors in 2021 were from underrepresented racial and ethnic groups.[6]

The most popular leadership authors and speakers are usually white men. They commonly offer how-tos and strategies for effective leadership that do not acknowledge the privilege that has contributed to their expertise. We are often given overly simplified lists, laws, and rules for what to do to be considered a good leader that gloss over the reality that many of us either cannot access those same behaviors and have a similar outcome or do not have the opportunity to exhibit those behaviors due to limiting work environments. Rhetoric centers on approaches that are not representative of our diverse experiences. Simplifying leadership into prescriptive, bite-sized how-tos demonstrates just how limited this view is. As leaders of color, we know a how-to does not exist for our realities—nor should there be, for effective leadership is much more complex in practice.

When we examine the state of leadership today, it is hard not to wonder if we have evolved much from that nineteenth-century theory. How have

UNTAPPED VOICES

I haven't read about how you challenge and change leadership by bringing different people in and empowering them. The examples of leadership stories in books are often very white or generalized—you don't hear about people with diverse or immigrant backgrounds. When you do, it's framed as if they were rare exceptions to the rest of their communities.

I would tell my younger self to be bolder and don't let others who don't look like you or have your experiences dictate what is acceptable in the workplace.

—Tammy, senior manager of an electric utility, Asian

we actually changed? We may cringe at the name and premise of great man theory, but that does not mean that we aren't still putting it in practice in subtle ways.

This critique is not to invalidate recent contributions to leadership discourse by those who represent the dominant culture; however, it reminds us that those perspectives do not represent or serve all of us. It highlights the urgency for new, more nuanced expertise from marginalized leaders to become part of this discourse *and* for it to be valued with the same credence afforded others. As we will explore, leaders of color offer expertise that everyone can learn from to become better leaders. We need to hear from those our society often overlooks.

TAP IN

What have you learned about leadership that you haven't read about from a book or heard from a speaker? What takeaways have you gathered from your own experience and observations?

SORTING, CATEGORIZING, AND VALUING
DOMINANT LEADERSHIP STYLES

Stemming from behavioral theories and with the ancillary backing of assessments like Myers-Briggs Type Indicator (MBTI), much ink has been spilled on how leaders should behave in order to be effective. We often evaluate "innate" leadership styles and preferences, finding it helpful to gain insight into our default behaviors and patterns of engaging with the world around us. What is not helpful is the subsequent sorting, categorizing, and ultimately valuing of various styles.

We have become accustomed to grouping people based on their personalities and behaviors. Doing so to deepen our understanding of typical behaviors may help us understand how to work with different types of people, particularly those who have different style preferences. However, it has become commonplace to attempt to predict certain outcomes or "stations" for different styles. Combined with the implicit biases that color how we believe we will or should act, and we have a recipe for a deeply embedded and pervasive issue: harmfully categorizing others largely based on assumptions. As we consider MBTI and how it has been used in employment decisions, subtle sorting processes likely have not benefited those with marginalized identities, relegating some into certain positions based on faulty presumptions about where they "naturally" belong.

Our minds are built for sorting information to make sense of it, especially when we have a lot to consider. We have to create meaning in a way that does not overtax our finite cognitive resources. So we categorize and make assumptions based on those categories. We pull from our past experiences, what we observe, and what we have been told to assess situations and decisions. At work, when we need to identify people who would be a good fit for certain roles, we attempt to predict success based on some of these style traits and expect others to perform in a way that aligns with how we have categorized them. In placing people in different roles, we attempt to play to their strengths, and to a certain extent, that process makes sense. We all have natural inclinations, and work becomes easier when we can utilize our strengths and exercise our preferences rather than working outside of or against them. Trouble arises when we define leadership by styles that typically stem from antiquated notions; for example, that leadership requires charisma, command, and control. This approach to leadership omits by default anyone without those qualities and behaviors, leading to more of the same.

Our society values gregarious verbal communicators: those who can command a room through speech tend to get the desired airspace, attention, and outcomes. Given power dynamics in many workspaces, such communicators are usually men who have more room to perform in such a manner thanks to our leadership roots. A 2004 study of Harvard law students found that men were 50 percent more likely to speak at least once in class than women and 144 percent more likely to speak three or more times.[7] That's a lot of airtime, which affects how those in the room consider who holds the influential weight of expressed knowledge and contribution. Inflated airtime leads to lopsided communication patterns; a George Washington University study showed that men interrupted women thirty-three times more often than when they were in conversation with other men.[8] It is common to hear stories of someone speaking over a team member during a meeting. There are, of course, dynamic exchanges in conversation—firm and formal dialogue boundaries also have limitations—however, when unnoticed or unchecked, these communication patterns can cultivate an environment that favors those who take the floor most often.

The term *mansplaining* emerged in recent decades, likely an outcome of this communication dynamic. Mansplaining refers to a phenomenon that occurs when men explain something, typically to women, often with a condescending tone and an assumption that the receiver is not knowledgeable on the subject (which often is incorrect). I've experienced it and witnessed it at work with a male colleague who offers his suggestions and direction on tasks that fall outside of his scope of responsibility and area of expertise. Although it can be benign—an effort to "help"—it ultimately undermines the perceived ability and expertise of the receiver. And though not limited to exchanges between men and women, the reality is that it evolved from centuries-old communication preferences. Although research explores this most explicitly as a gender dynamic, we should be interested in learning if similar patterns emerge in exchanges in which entrenched societal power dynamics such as race are present.

Dynamics such as mansplaining and gendered interrupting patterns are effective at muting voices and demotivating contributions from others in the

UNTAPPED VOICES

I was encouraged by some of my managers to take more responsibility, be more in charge, only to feel that if I don't conform to their idea of how that looks like, I fail. If I emulated their behavior, it felt like some defenses get triggered and I was interrupted, talked over, or habitually my conclusion couldn't be the last one. It would often be paraphrased to finish a discussion. This mixed signaling was very confusing and took a toll on my confidence. So I found myself juggling an incentive to conform to an expected style of leadership, imposter syndrome, and desire for a different style of leadership or rather freedom of leadership expression (that could be measured by the traditional KPIs [key performance indicators]).

—Elena, executive, music licensing, Asian

room. So too are the instances when someone offers an idea that's initially overlooked, only to have a colleague repeat it later to a more cognizant reception. Underlying these exchanges is a value we give these behaviors: if we allow it, we value it, and by the widespread nature of these phenomena, evidently, we value interruptions and interrupters enough to allow the commonplace behavior. We should remain cognizant of the connections to the ideas proposed by great man theory that permeate professional discourse and communication preferences. Compare how many publications advise introverts on how to assert themselves with those that instruct extroverts how to pause or pull back, and we can see the bias. The leadership deficit is assumed to occur mostly among those who may not jump out in front, at first, or at all.

We often expect individuals at the tops of our organizations to be visionary and inspiring. They exude confidence, which garners trust in their leadership and inspires us to look to them for hope and direction in our future. It's comforting. It's motivating. It's important. However, if we *only* look to these individuals for leadership and overlook other leaders with different communications styles and strengths, then we limit our interpretation of who we believe is capable of leading.

Verbal communicators, extroverts, drivers, and challengers are prioritized in traditional leadership frameworks. "Command and control" is sometimes dismissed as an outdated leadership approach, but it remains active in the modern workplace and plays out in different ways. Those atop organizations oftentimes implement top-down policies to ensure that their workforce adheres to their responsibilities rather than trusting and observing that they are. We saw command and control play out in a number of ways when much of the white-collar workforce worked from home during the COVID-19 pandemic. Some in positions of authority, in response to a weakened level of control, instituted policies requiring cameras to be on during virtual meetings and setting increased communication expectations to keep tabs on team members. We see command and control play out in micro-management scenarios in which managers not only dictate "the what" of their employees' work, but also "the how." More subtly, however, we see command and control emerge indirectly as those with the loudest or most frequent voices garner attention and influence for their own ideas and direction.

Leadership is assigned to those who can command and ultimately control the vision, narrative, outcome, and bottom line. Their ideas are weighted heavier than others because they are expressed with gusto. We are accustomed to leadership frameworks that center on moving others toward an outcome. The process or the people themselves are not essential. What results is leadership that misses marginalized voices and can exclude others implicitly or explicitly by virtue of leaders' preferences for a certain type of team member or their narrow focus on final outcomes.

HEROES ON PEDESTALS

We have examined ideas of leaders as heroes, leadership requiring followers, and leadership as determined by behaviors, traits, and situations, but we have not explored much beyond those parameters. When we tell stories of historical leaders, we tend to *heroize* them. We like the hero. We root for the protagonist. Beginning in elementary school, we read about heroes in make-believe stories that make us all want to save the day to the applause of everyone looking on. We begin to create deep-seated values around heroic leadership at a very young age, which is later cultivated in our search for real-life heroes to applaud: elected officials, company presidents, and even Hollywood celebrities can find themselves cast in that role whether they auditioned for it or not.

Given the status that we assign to those roles, we expect these individuals to continually earn that status through their knowledge, expert decision making, and unerring direction. One misstep and that status is at risk of being revoked. Such unforgiving terms are completely unrealistic, for every single one of us has made mistakes big and small throughout our careers. Yet we apply increased scrutiny to leaders' decisions because we have placed so much onus on them having all the answers.

This heroic interpretation of leadership is not sustainable. No one can meet these expectations, yet, thus far, we have been committed to them. It is not sustainable for leaders in the racial or gender majority, and even less so for marginalized leaders already burdened by the weight of navigating societal hierarchies. The foundation of leadership is faulty in ways beyond its exclusion of untapped voices. It harms the entire system and our society as a whole.

When examining this critically to expose the nuances of this interpretation, we find connections grounded in our nation's history. A select few, the leader-heroes, are out in front or on top, making decisions on behalf of the rest of us. The idea of *hero* implies *few*, reinforcing a limiting definition of leadership that excludes almost everyone.

As we build up leader-heroes in our perceptions, they evolve from humans who undoubtedly make mistakes into impermeable, untouchable individuals who can withstand anything—or at least, that is what is expected. The room for grace thins, and the list of expectations widens. It is a tall order to satisfy, and disappointment is inevitable. In creating structures that rely on singular leaders or a select group at the top of organizational hierarchies to make the big decisions, we have sown seeds that will yield an unstable crop. This unsustainable practice watches us fill top positions with person after unsuccessful person without considering if or how the organization could be led by many.

We remain attached to this heroic leadership idea nonetheless. It limits our ability to think systemically because we often look to the leader, an individualistic lens that minimizes what leadership could actually be. We need to divest from conflating leadership with heroism and we can do so first by leading with transparency, collaboration, and trust and by releasing control. We also need to be received with graciousness and forgiveness during the inevitable moments when we falter. Not only does this immediately affect anyone marginalized in traditional leadership frameworks, but it also creates an environment in which everyone can thrive within their realistic best.

THE UNREALISTIC ASK FOR COMPARTMENTALIZATION

In a leadership class during my doctoral studies, I remember reading *The Leadership Challenge* by Jim Kouzes and Barry Posner as part of the course's assigned reading. (To note, the syllabus included only publications written by white men.) As a result of hundreds of thousands of surveys and interviews, they found that good leaders model behavior, inspire a shared vision, challenge processes, enable teams, and celebrate the accomplishments of others.[9] I recall reading the brief book and thinking, *That's it?* I understood that the book's simplicity was intentional and effective in creating something digestible from wide and deep research data sets, yet its conclusions did not feel accessible or simple. At least not for me. As a woman of color, I need to tread carefully when challenging a process; for example, harmful tropes such as the "angry Black woman" can persevere within workplace biases. The other aspects of good leadership made sense, and I agreed with them. Yet I recall an overall sense of deflation; the one-dimensional nature of the advice would not be easy to implement for someone navigating the workplace with marginalized identities. What I did not realize then was that I was inherently picking up on the fact that more than 75 percent of participants in the research were white.[10] Ultimately, I felt there was something missing from my own leadership journey, which may have been because the data were largely informed by perspectives that differed from my own.

These reflections are not to discount the leadership research contributions of Kouzes and Posner nor the general relevancy and resonance of the takeaways. However, *The Leadership Challenge* illuminated to me that some are afforded the opportunity to lead without worry or awareness of societal realities. In these cases, leading is simplified when one's social identity does not add layers of complexity to navigate. The five practices of leadership may very well be core tenets of the field, but the calculus to get there differs based on context. The practices become more accessible as the factors in the equation simplify. For those who identify with dominant culture, the concept of "checking things at the door" and leading fully within tenets such as these is feasible because there is simply less to check at the door.

The ability to compartmentalize typically has been deemed as a strength. A widely accepted assumption is that the better you become at separating work from life (or even you as a person from you as an employee), the more effective you are as a leader. We compartmentalize to better perform our roles. We send our polished representative and not our true, messy selves because that is what is expected and that is what gets rewarded.

The morning when I returned to work after the birth of my first child was complete chaos. I pumped as much milk as I could and tried to eat something. I dressed and tried to look semiprofessional, as if I had slept for more than two-hour blocks during the past four months. I said an emotional goodbye with my baby and left the house, struck by the significance of the identity shift I had just gone through. I tackled the impossible Los Angeles rush-hour commute, walked into my office, and pushed everything aside, showing up as expected.

Internally, however, I was in shock that the world expected so much of me. How is this realistic? How can we expect anyone to leave their bags at the door and to create such distance between what they are experiencing and feeling and what is expected of them at work? The effort to compartmentalize during that time was a heavy burden. It felt unfair and was, in fact, unfair.

Because leadership research and rhetoric stemmed from white men, we can assume their perspectives developed the norms and expectations of professional work. This expectation to compartmentalize stems from these dominant norms: they have less distance to travel between who they are and how they must show up at work. The intersections of race, gender, ability, and other social identities place fewer burdens on those around whom leadership structures have been centered and built. They are afforded the space to ingest simplified leadership lessons and put them into immediate practice because they do not carry the challenges and complexities that others have.

Compartmentalization is even more strenuous in recent decades with the 24/7, always-on culture of work and information. The current nature of

TAP IN

What aspects of yourself are marginalized at work? What gets "checked at the door" for the sake of professionalism, collaboration, and maintaining credibility? What might be missed in the case for creativity, innovation, and critical analysis of complex work challenges if we don't access or offer all of our available information?

work is a boundary-free setup. We can be accessed at any time via email, cell phone, and even our watches. Work comes home with us, on vacation, and, sadly, to doctors' offices and hospitals. We are tied to inboxes and available through chat functions almost twenty-four hours a day. We often extend ourselves beyond comfortable capacity to keep up, and there is no sign of that demand alleviating. The nature of leadership today calls for mental, emotional, and physical labor that seems to be always increasing. To lead within this culture is taxing, for effective and impactful leadership requires energy, and energy is finite.

MOVING BEYOND DIVERSITY, EQUITY, AND INCLUSION

Despite necessary discussions on diversity, equity, and inclusion (DEI), none of it acknowledges the reality that our core still stems from a problematic tree. As we witness DEI efforts become ancillary or performative within many organizations, I can only point to our shaky foundation of leadership. Organizations often call in facilitators and consultants or even an executive-level team member to focus on the company's DEI initiatives. Yet we soon discover a lack of depth or real change behind the lip service, the limited structural change, and the burnt-out DEI executives who have hit the walls given the impossibility of the task. In essence we are just adding branches to our trunk.

Effective diversity, equity, and inclusion efforts actually require the reframing of what we consider to be leadership. We need to work on the roots, not the branches. As disorienting as that might be, it is necessary for the health of our organizations' leadership. Companies' top executives and boards can no longer hold narrow, singular perspectives of the social realities of our current world. Prioritizing predominantly white male perspectives in leadership rhetoric indirectly but impactfully influences our interpretations of leadership in the day-to-day work. Those who align in identity and approach are favored, and those who differ receive fewer opportunities to exercise their own leadership approaches to achieve increased authority in an organization.

UPROOTING MISLEADERSHIP

We don't often recognize the connection between the dominant perspectives consumed via airport reads and business school classes and the lack of representation in top roles, but the connection is there. Implicit and even explicit biases grow in this type of environment. We not only absorb the message and the "single story" being shared by this subset of society, but we also take in the images of the storytellers. A bias develops toward those perspectives because they are familiar and abundant. We unquestionably accept that these experts are where they should be, and when we see the same in our organizations, we don't second-guess their status. These stories are viewed as accurate representations of effective leadership, so we want those who align in behavior and physicality to lead our organizations because we are repeatedly told that they can—a not-so-subtle reinforcement of exclusionary rhetoric.

The definition of *misleading* is "giving someone the wrong idea or impression." We are not always initially aware of when we are being misled. It could be a startup pitch with lofty yet believable promises, as we've seen from Silicon Valley at times. Or the membership service that promotes an enticing price only to reveal its true self in the small-print details. If we remain vigilant, we can catch on to misleading offers before signing up, but sometimes we unknowingly subscribe. We are accustomed to discussing the concept of being misled as a verb, but we are not accustomed to recognizing *misleadership* as a noun.

Misleadership describes the limited and limiting definitions of what we currently consider leadership. Grounded in frameworks developed by a dominant group studying the leadership traits, behaviors, and decisions of others in the same group, these theories carry excessive weight in leadership rhetoric despite their limited perspective. Essentially writing about themselves, they use language that resonates with only some of us. The rest of us must stretch, bend, and contort to make it fit when we know deep down those interpretations are not us. We can fall to this misleadership when we are set up to believe that we are not up to the task these frameworks posit, when in fact they may not capture the full essence of our leadership challenge. True leadership requires context and a deep awareness of the complete picture, something lacking in the current leadership landscape.

Although this misleadership could be unintentional, a conscious choice is being made regarding who defines leadership today. There is pervasive complicity in not questioning why a dominant group primarily defines the field. That preservation of who defines leadership subtly underlines where and by whom power is held. If the definition of leadership were broadened and included different approaches and purposes, power would undoubtedly shift. We all are misled because we are not digging into the depths of possibility of what leadership can be. We haven't sifted through the caveats included in the fine print.

Leadership researchers, authors, and practitioners must acknowledge their role in perpetuating the lack of representation of women and BIPOC leaders in top positions due to the limited and limiting nature of the current definitions. Going beyond inclusion, an overhaul of this nature calls for mics to be passed and spotlights to be shifted. This book and the expanded perspectives shared are the first steps, but we have centuries to go in order to catch up on everything we have missed since the 1800s.

It's not always clear when a tree is in poor health. There may be signs of decay in its roots before it shows elsewhere. It can be difficult to pinpoint at times, but it is essential to do so before a tree's decay results in harm to a person or structure nearby when it topples over, because it will ultimately topple over. We are at the point now where we need to acknowledge that the proverbial leadership tree is not healthy—not because present leadership narratives are in themselves diseased, but because the tree as a whole has not been planted in the most nutrient-rich soil possible to allow it to fully thrive. Not all perspectives have been cultivated in that soil. Leaders of color have

UNTAPPED VOICES

I'm of a very strong belief by now that there is really no right or wrong way to lead. There are different ways to lead, but we're so anchored and biased by the traditional way that anything that deviates from it, whether it's a self-imposed feeling or we get that reaction from others, might feel like we're not fit for leadership. And that's what I'm challenging. I'm challenging how we define success. I'm challenging how we get to success. We need to expand the range of how success looks and feels.

—Elena, executive, music licensing, Asian

not been able to contribute their expertise to the same extent as others. As a result, our tree is weakened and more susceptible to the elements. Our organizations and systems remain battered as a result of crisis after crisis, bracing nervously for the next, and yet we haven't utilized all available assets to move us through.

3

THE LIMITATIONS OF LEADERSHIP TODAY

In 2021 following George Floyd's murder and a racial awakening that seemed to spring up across the United States, organizations scrambled to respond in support of diversity, equity, and inclusion efforts. Some had been working toward more diverse and equitable workplaces for decades. Others were like deer in headlights, operating without awareness of or interest in developing work cultures that were inclusive of their diverse teams. Some scrambled to react, creating performative efforts to signal their commitment but without following through with actual structural change. It was uncomfortable to witness, yet the moment for that level of critical awareness and inquiry was welcomed because exclusive and inequitable workplaces were even more uncomfortable.

Amid the onslaught of Black and brown faces catapulted into advertising campaigns, one commercial's message stood out as I considered what that moment meant for work and leadership even as I eye-rolled these late, superficial efforts. Proctor & Gamble debuted a short that was titled "Widen the Screen—A Fuller Picture of Black Life." It began with snippets of Black people in everyday scenarios: two teenagers entering a convenience store with a white store owner looking on; a pregnant young mother struggling to carry a grocery bag and the toddler in her arms, an older child walking nearby; a man wearing a cap and gold chain driving an old Cadillac down the street, arriving at a home after dark. With each scenario, there is a purposeful pause as the short's director lets the audience's assumptions pile up.

Another teenager wearing a hoodie that hides his face enters the convenience store as the shop owner flashes a look of concern; the young mother waits in the parking lot with her bags and children; the man knocks loudly on the door of the home, glancing over his shoulder. We mentally fill in the blanks with scenes that play out time and time again in films and television: the teenager shoplifts, the young woman is a single mother, and the man is breaking into the home. Our biases run wild—instantly.

What happens then is the beauty of this short. The screen widens, and we see the full picture. The teenager enters the store, laughs and high fives his friends, and, of course, *pays* the smiling shop owner as Black teenagers do. A minivan pulls up near the young mother, whose partner takes the bag and excited kids in his arms. The man at the door is greeted with a huge smile and big hug and ushered into a vibrant house filled with people sharing a meal. It was a stark reminder of the danger of narrowing our lenses, particularly when only certain narratives have been told by a dominant culture.

The premise behind the P&G ad addresses an important issue: when limiting our view of anything—whether it be media intake, reading material, or definitions of leadership—we run the risk of either falsely believing we see the full picture despite our limited lens or taking liberties in completing that picture ourselves based on past experiences or what we have witnessed before. In leadership, if we continue to build from a limited foundation, then we are operating within the same problematic window. Through examining the state of leadership today and seeing the glaring lack of representation in top organizational roles, it becomes clear that we are unaware of what lies beyond our limited screen or that we are choosing not to look.

The pervasive limitations of how we interpret leadership emerge subtly in our language and symbols, all reinforcing the shoddy foundation and weak roots from which we have built the current framework. As we examine the source of our definitions, their interpretations, and their connected trajectory to present-day methods, we can notice how narrowly we've operated in our practice of leadership. We did not begin with the full picture—on purpose—and we have not committed to examining the full picture even today.

FROM TRIANGLES TO CIRCLES

When we think about leadership, we undoubtedly conjure triangular imagery. We imagine a narrow top with a broad base. There is typically one person at the very top with a small, select group of others on the rung below; from there the structure widens, with the largest number of people at the very bottom. We often include this image on organizational charts, drawing lines between the rungs to indicate supervisory relationships and to solidify our visual representation of where leadership sits.

Our hierarchical organizations stem from those nineteenth-century interpretations of what makes a solid work structure. We have discussed our enthusiasm for the idea of leaders heroically guiding us from the top. The onus is placed on the leaders to offer the rest of us vision and direction: they reached the top of the pyramid, so we assume they hold the knowledge and ability to stably hold the structure together. These commonplace triangular structures imply that this is the ideal and only model to consider for effective organizations.

In that imagery and in practice, however, power becomes deeply embedded into the system itself, creating the assumption that the only way to hold power is to make it to the top. Of course, the likelihood of making it to the top is low among those with marginalized identities, and in that reality lies our problematic narrow lens. What if triangular hierarchical structures are not the strongest operational designs for our organizations? What if we explored circular imagery when thinking about what effective leadership requires and what impactful organizations embody?

It is not by chance that we don't imagine leadership as a circular, all-encompassing model, for it doesn't align with our foundational definitions and frameworks. If we were to consider a circular model of leadership, we would place the purpose or mission at the center with leaders orchestrating the interplay within that circle. This interconnected web may include executive-level participants who likely play an important role, but it would widen to include many others who facilitate the success of the collective vision. In this model, leadership is distributed; it is dynamic and fluid, not static and confined to the top. In fact, there is no top. This concept is challenging to imagine, and more questions than answers might emerge regarding how such a leadership structure could work. Nevertheless, the leadership needed today requires frames that include rather than exclude most.

SCARCITY MODELS OF LEADERSHIP

When we reference the "leadership of the organization," we often refer to those at the top with the most positional authority. The phrase is used so often that we don't even think critically about it. Leadership is synonymous with "the top." That is all we have known, and that knowledge has permeated the nonchalant way we reference "the leadership" even in scenarios in which real leadership isn't being exercised in those top rungs. In my work with midcareer professionals across all sectors, I have lost count of how many times someone referenced the "leadership" of their organization and then went on to describe textbook toxic behaviors from those "leaders."

We have not divorced leadership from titles and levels of authority, and that is causing us to miss out on so much more. Rather than considering "the leadership" as occurring at all levels, we apply the reference to only a handful that, again, are usually not representative of our diverse society. It is fascinating to listen to people discuss the leadership of their organizations with a sense of annoyance and disappointment without thinking to refer to those executives as something else. The compulsion to call them "leaders" runs deep.

Using language in this way is powerful for our subconscious. It places leadership *over there* with someone else and not within oneself. It limits our beliefs. It constricts our understanding of leadership. To equate hierarchical authority so swiftly and so broadly with leadership proves how far we have to go to unlearn these deeply embedded interpretations. If we define leadership this way, we reserve the title of leader for only a select and predictable few, because we know from the data that leaders of color are less likely to be included in that subset of society.

Our language and symbols rely on a scarcity model of leadership wherein only a few can be considered leaders. If we audit how we visualize and consider leadership—in small ways we may not realize or that we outwardly reject yet tacitly internalize—we see how exclusionary our current models can be. We not only create triangular images of leaders at the top with everyone else at the bottom, but we also place leaders in front and the rabble in the

---

TAP IN

If we believed that leadership existed at all levels of our organizations—not just at the top—how would we restructure our practices to acknowledge, cultivate, and reward it? What elements of our current practices and culture would need to change?

---

back; experts lead, and novices follow. We set up conceptual structures that by design marginalize many from accessing these positions, withholding the title of leader until it is earned with time and status. Earned, yes, but also bestowed upon us by others, usually in ways that are prescribed by how we define leadership. In a culture of scarcity and competition, this is no easy feat.

Assuming that not everyone can be a leader, the only way to take hold of this distinction is to stand out in some way. This can be in title, authority, charisma, intelligence, or other distinguishing factors. Although these components may be unobjectionable in and of themselves, lauding them as the most salient aspects of leadership ultimately limits us. We have defined and discussed leadership so narrowly that only a few are able to stand out from the crowd and lead the many toward an identified purpose.

This model of perceived scarcity has deep roots in the foundation of leadership and exposes the limited progress we have made in the field. By limiting access to leadership, the word becomes a gatekeeping title with many on a quest to improve their skills in that area through courses, books, and coaching. Rather than interpreting leadership as something we exercise, we lean toward defining it as something we *are*. As soon as we begin to assign the title to people or to internalize our own interpretations of who is a leader and who is not, we begin to narrow the scope of our lens. At times, with implicit biases at play, that narrowing can become problematic, and we tell the story before it plays out, as the P&G commercial exposed.

We do not approach our definitions of leadership with a wide-angle lens. We look through phone cameras when we should be watching big-screen action through a movie-grade cinema camera. We have created stories for the characters on screen, in our workplaces, and in our lives, because our histories have written the narratives for those characters long before we even experience them. Once we determine the main characters of films and television shows, everyone else must serve in a supporting capacity, because we believe there can be only a small number of lead characters. Everything that we visualize is seen through a scarcity definition of leadership. It cannot exist in many places, in many ways, and through many people at once, because if it did, we might then argue that it is not leadership. To challenge that assumption, we need to widen our screens, expand our lenses, and restructure our sets. What would it look like if leadership narratives were built around the idea of ensemble casts, where each character offers a unique contribution, and no one person is the star? What added depth and nuance could we discover as each person garners similar camera attention and offers balanced levels of contribution? Otherwise, without this shift, we will continue operating within a scarcity mindset that reserves access to leadership for a select few, and historically we've seen that it usually falls in line with the dominant culture's definition of who deserves that access.

LEADERSHIP IS POWER, AND POWER IS LIMITED . . . ALLEGEDLY

Since we conflate positional authority with leadership, we cannot imagine those in power as anything but "the leadership"—of the team, organization, country, or movement. We equate power with leadership; they are one and the same. We cannot examine the limitations of leadership today without also assessing our perceptions of power. As we have explored, the inequitable distribution of power in our broader society also exists within our leadership structures. The latter, in fact, helps prop up the former. They inform and sustain each other.

If we consider power a finite resource, we can critically examine how and when it is used, by whom, and for what purpose. Given our deeply embedded leadership frameworks that place leaders at the top and in charge, we give a lot of power to those in leadership positions, or they may wield power knowing that their position affords them the right to do so. We don't question how much power those whom we define as leaders have over us, but we should. We witnessed increased questioning of power and equity in 2020, which has been an essential practice in strengthening our society, and we

UNTAPPED VOICES

I think that, as leaders, we don't grapple with the power that we actually have. We have a tenuous, uncomfortable, and dishonest relationship with power. We only see and experience power as "power over'" as the primary expression of what a leader is in the context of the work world. Because we don't access power with "power to" or "power within" frameworks, we have a very binary either/or thinking approach to understanding what leadership is and is not.

—Merle, CEO of a national nonprofit, Black

have the opportunity to continue to intentionally examine its pervasiveness in our mundane day-to-day reality.

With the understanding that power is limited, assigning that finite resource to a select few is limiting for all of us. With a narrow lens of leadership, we also then have a narrow lens of the formal power that leadership often offers. Formal power is decision-making authority granted to someone based on a formal position, title, or job description. For example, executives exercise formal power as a result of the authority they have been granted by virtue of their position. The more authority, the more power, the more consequential their decisions will be on behalf of others. Since we currently situate leadership at this very top of organizational structures, this assigned formal power is often how we "see" leadership. Power is the observable output that we can more easily grasp. Once someone is out of that leadership position, that person's formal power goes away or shifts to whatever new form of authority the individual holds. Thus, formal power stays with the role and not with the person, which then weakens the argument that leadership is unquestionably connected to formal power and authority.

With a broader view of leadership, we build a broader view of power as well. Recalling the circular model of leadership, for example, we could imagine a more distributive sense of power that centers not on one person's vision, but on a collective purpose. This model breaks up the limited definition of power and expands it exponentially by acknowledging and leveraging the power we all hold.

It would be naive to think that power does not play a significant role in our quest for and experience with leadership. Our surface-level analysis assumes honorable intentions motivate our desire to lead, but the pursuit of personal power often drives our desire for leadership as we currently define it. The power afforded to those in leadership positions also comes with particular societal benefits, whether or not the leaders are considered to be effective in actual leadership. They typically have increased professional autonomy, increased pay, and even improved treatment in the workplace, because no one wants to cross the boss. Anyone would want that kind of freedom, so it is understandable fuel for the pursuit of leadership roles.

Within this interplay between power and leadership lies the boundary lines of how one can or will operate as a leader. Given the privileges afforded to those in leadership, we can predict that those in such positions would want to maintain and preserve those benefits. The surefire way to do this is to stay in line and conduct themselves and assert their authority according to the leadership scholarship of the last one-hundred-plus years—often through centralized decision making, knowledge-holding gatekeeping, and exclusion.

UNTAPPED VOICES

It's critical to hold an awareness of and exercise responsible use of power. I've been in organizations that were trying to be very flat and nonhierarchical from a philosophical standpoint—very social justice oriented. I really appreciated the ethos. But the reality is that there was a hierarchy and there were power dynamics and they just weren't being named. If they're not named, they can't be tamed. There can't be checks and balances to power that's not named. You need to have clarity around what each person's role is, what decisions they are responsible for, and what's your sphere of power and influence versus somebody else's. It needs to be very clear and transparent so it can be balanced. In the absence of that, there's more likely to be abuses of power and mistrust that percolates.

—Sara, self-employed in strategic operations
and culture design, South Asian

THE IMPOSSIBILITY OF RESILIENT LEADERSHIP

In lockstep with our expectations of leaders as unfazed heroes in the face of uncertainty and tumult, a line of leadership rhetoric has begun to focus on the necessity of resilience. Our world is increasingly more challenging. It seems as if the rules of engagement are ever-changing, the nature of work has shifted to a new reality, and resilience seems to be a prerequisite to leading through this shift. We are called to withstand change and remain steady against headwinds and full-blown tornados. Supposedly we more readily achieve success when we are impervious to stormy conditions and can guide others with clarity and confidence as if we are unaffected by the elements. Any outward signs that suggest we are superhuman can only help us move toward success. In these uncertain environments, it is no wonder we place such an emphasis on resilience as a leadership trait.

In theory, I understand the need for resiliency in leadership. Leaders often carry a sizable load of responsibilities, making decisions within rapidly and unexpectedly changing environments. At some point, they disappoint or fail to meet expectations because they are real humans, not fictional heroes. If leaders were knocked back by everything that came toward them, progress would be minimal. Outcomes would likely not be met. Teams might operate with misdirection and confusion. So yes, resilience plays a definite role in leadership.

In practice, though, the call for resilient leadership comes with limitations, as it is not always sustainable or feasible. In fact, it might ultimately affect our ability to lead impactfully during moments when we've armored to respond unfazed to damaging realities when they may actually call for us to heed to our human limitations. Resilience is a steep ask at this point. Leadership and resilience before 2020 were a different level than the times we have navigated since. The scope, scale, and speed at which the need for resilience erupts are considerably greater. We have navigated a deadly pandemic, political polarization that fueled an insurrection at the Capitol, traumatic school shootings, and racial violence—all while figuring out how to return to in-person work in a hybrid world. These have not been normal times, and any signs of so-called resilience at this point likely teeter on the edge of robotic.

There is something about resiliency that conjures images of steel walls and impermeability. "When the going gets tough, the tough get going," as the saying goes. The distance between the world and the heart stretches to create the space needed to bounce back and persevere because the work outcomes need it. Right? At least, we have decided that they do. It doesn't feel realistic in our current state, nor does it feel appropriate. Current expectations of leadership repudiate the systemic weaknesses that exist. We are called to respond resiliently and continuously, but that expectation is not doing anyone any good.

It has been well documented that the COVID-19 pandemic has taken a toll on working mothers, for example. Mothers were often doubly burdened with work responsibilities, childcare duties, and heavier household loads.[1] What is being exposed are the unrealistic expectations for mothers to show up at the same level or above as their counterparts without children. This issue also sheds light on an untenable childcare system often held together by underpaid and overworked childcare providers that are concurrently quite expensive or unavailable due to limited options. Let us also not forget the entrenched and persistent gender dynamic that cultivates an inequitable load of which women often bear the brunt. The task is herculean, and the articles covering these experiences seem to always note these moms' resiliency. Their capacity stretches, the balls are juggled, and it all still gets done. But at what cost? And for what purpose? To keep these systemic and societal failures tethered together?

We are doing more than should be necessary and adding too much armor onto the essence of what makes us human, which is actually what is needed for effective leadership. By the same token, we are limiting some of the keen senses that allow us to utilize emotion and feeling in decision making. We are powering through during moments when we should power down. In the name of resilience, we are not spending enough time grieving and connecting meaningfully with others because we have always been told that those emotions need to be shed for us to lead. We have muted essential parts of ourselves—and our leadership—in these moments because we are not allowing ourselves to fully acknowledge the ways in which the world is not okay. We get tough, and we get going, complicitly perpetuating our troubles because our banner of resilience tells us we can and should handle it.

Rather than focusing on building resilient leaders, we should focus on building resilient systems, ones that can distribute and better hold the burden. Ones that are flexible and responsive and can change when the moment calls for it. Ones that are also stable and reliable because they have been built on trust, authenticity, and connection. Relying on a single leader to be resilient is not a sustainable or effective solution. It is a setup that undoubtedly limits effectiveness when such unrealistic expectations are placed on fallible, feeling individuals. We are using individual resiliency to sustain what are actually systemic weaknesses, and that practice does not promote longevity for the individual or the system. It is a Band-Aid fix at the cost of our most marginalized communities when we should be fortifying the underlying structure. Though these communities are disproportionately affected adversely by broken systems, everyone suffers under such an unrealistic and unsustainable expectation for resilience.

If we think about the walls and barriers we envision when speaking of resilience, those references are better aligned with structures than with people, yet we apply them to leadership because of the unattainable and unsustainable traits and behaviors we look for in our leaders. It is another example of limiting misinterpretations of what leadership should be. Although resilient leadership plays a role—in how you recover from mistakes; in how you accept difficult but accurate, constructive feedback; in how you pivot willingly when necessary—it becomes a liability when you carry the world's burdens and conceal how much the weight is bringing you down too.

THE PREDICTABILITY OF TOXIC LEADERSHIP

Much ink has been spilled and much discussion had on the subject of toxic leadership. There are stories of toxic leaders who are demeaning to others, who engage in unprofessional workplace gossip, who pit team members against each other, and who generally devolve the trust of an organization through their interpersonal mismanagement. Yet running concurrently to these behaviors is their ability to produce. Despite their toxic behaviors, they are often considered performers or even rock stars.

The fact that we still use "leadership" in conjunction with the word "toxic" reveals much about what we value and how we define the former term. Despite their destructive behavior, these people qualify as leaders either because (1) they are in a position of authority and we associate leadership with the top of the pyramid structure, or (2) we value the outcome enough to disregard the means of achieving it. "Toxic leadership" should be an oxymoron, yet we encounter the phrase everywhere. When we allow and even reward toxic leadership in our workplaces, we double down on our commitment to misunderstanding leadership. Those who reference examples of toxic leadership at work are often the same people who complain that nothing is done to reprimand those individuals. Toxic interpersonal exchanges have no consequences because the work product takes precedence. It is not uncommon to see these individuals given more responsibility, more authority, and more opportunity to continue their problematic practices, because promotion increases their privileges.

Similar to how we equate leadership with power, we confuse "leadership" with "level of work output." Rather than recognizing toxic team members as inhibiting progress and missing a critical element of successful leadership, we instead excuse those glaring gaps for the sake of the bottom line or mission. This toxicity not only severely limits the leadership potential of others (because toxic leaders are usually not inclusive), but it shrinks the space for leading with integrity (because integrity is ultimately undermined in a toxic environment).

UNTAPPED VOICES

Professionally most individuals and executive teams at organizations are too often unwilling to have hard and difficult conversations. They shy away from conflict and view it as a negative thing rather than being willing to do the hard work of engaging with employees and colleagues, encouraging multiple viewpoints, and having a commitment to supporting teams through conflict rather than just avoiding it. This can lead to environments of mistrust, secrecy, and toxicity within organizations. This also can result in employees feeling like mistakes should be hidden or avoided, which can most definitely affect growth and learning.

—Clara, director, philanthropy, Latinx

Given the foundations of leadership we have built, the structures we use to maintain that foundation, and the language and symbols we use to communicate these deep-seated values, the prevalence of toxic leadership is predictable. It can exist only in a structure that places leadership at the top of a homogenous hierarchy of very few. It creates a success-at-all-costs dynamic that often runs unchecked. It clearly communicates what behaviors are rewarded in practice even as we tout tenets of authentic, inclusive, and empathetic leadership. In an environment ruled by toxic leadership, those traits and behaviors are undervalued at best and unwelcome at worst.

THE POWER OF IMAGES AND LANGUAGE

When it comes to how we consider leadership, we underestimate the power of images and language. Each word we use and every diagram we create communicates certain leadership values that are important to us. We are not without broader interpretations about how leaders should show up, for there have been countless books on authentic leadership, empathetic leadership, introverted leadership, and almost any type of leadership we can think of. However, our go-to symbols and language expose what is salient to our definition of leadership. We can theorize and expand narratives, but our foundation, our core, our narrowed lens remains the same in practice.

We are comfortable with and possibly resigned to our pyramidic and individualistic interpretations of what leadership is. In working toward earning our turn on those topmost desirable rungs, we are missing out on the leadership we possess and can exercise in this moment. We overlook what is possible at different career and life stages because we have not widened the lens to see beyond what has always been in view. Our systems have also remained narrow, corralling us within antiquated models of command-and-control leadership structures that often remain subversively present in management practices and decision-making structures. As these systems are failing and failing fast, we need to explore what else is possible.

Leadership without an understanding of context is not leadership. Real leadership keeps a constant critical lens on the status quo it perpetuates and requires an expansive definition that decenters power imbalances and superiority. What is missing across leadership research is the acknowledgment, and more likely awareness, of the role that social dynamics such as race play in the workplace and how that can shape what effective leadership requires. It's undoubtedly hard to simplify such complexity into brief principles or a symbolic diagram. At the very least, however, acknowledgment of those complex realities should be the baseline from which we start.

Publications that have overlooked the impact of social dynamics through simplified models have served as the canon in classrooms, management programs, and executive suites training the next generation of leaders in ways that do not fully encompass the reality they'll face regardless of demographic. The story is flawed without the inclusion of more voices—others in the ensemble or, better yet, behind the camera—contributing leadership perspectives on equal footing as those traditionally identified as the stars of the show. Leadership needs to be reimagined for real progress and organizational success to be achieved, and we'll shift that authority in the coming pages.

TAP IN

If you were to scrub all of the standard, expected language used to describe leadership and rewrite it fully as your most casual, comfortable, and authentic self, how would you describe it?

Language carries weight. If we are not utilizing our own words and phrases to describe leadership but are instead adopting inherited language, how would decoding toward more familiar descriptors impact our proximity to our own leadership?

4

A NECESSARY SHIFT IN LEADERSHIP AUTHORITY

Now that we have a clearer idea of the substantial representation gaps in current and past leadership frameworks, we need to shift our focus toward understanding and valuing the perspectives of those sidelined in traditional leadership frameworks. As we widen our lens and create a more complete and real picture, we undoubtedly learn from those who approach leadership from a different societal standpoint.

As pedestals are erected and heroes are accorded with accolades and criticism—sometimes in the same breath—distance is created between a leader and everyone else. It is systematic and expected. Leaders are said to have thirty-thousand-foot views and understanding, and although there is value in that view, a lot is also missed.

It can and has been argued that those on lower rungs of our social hierarchies are better positioned to understand the true nature of human relations and social realities. The standpoint of BIPOC leaders brings a more layered understanding of critical work challenges and offers leadership approaches more connected to reality than those whose dominant perspectives may cause them to miss or choose to disregard the whole picture.

UNTAPPED VOICES

When I was growing up in the '80s and '90s, I was pushed to conform both to white American society and also my parents' over-idealized memories of Muslim Bengali culture (they left Bangladesh when they were sixteen in the early '70s). At times, of course, even my parents' preferences conflicted with other direction they were giving me (be an independent, highly educated woman vs. don't be too smart or you'll never get a husband—literally both told to me by my mother the night before I left for college at Harvard). At some point I realized I couldn't please everyone, so I started to listen to myself.

Through a process that is still ongoing, I began interrogating my values, what is actually meaningful and motivating to me, and what/ how to communicate this to people I care about or those who have expectations of me. What I've found is that this process has led to my strength in understanding others' goals/motivations and an ability to resolve tension, disagreements, or confusion with empathy and clarity. Not only has this led to my personal success in my own business, but it has also informed the very way we operate as a business. Our core values define the kind of work we do, the people we serve, and how we mentor both students and employees.

This kind of cultural and people competency could only have been possible through my experience growing up as a first-generation American—so as much of a struggle as it was (and has been) to deal with model minority myths, parental/cultural pressures, racism, and the ups and downs that come with finding oneself through exploration and experimentation, there is a real strength and resilience that has come out of it. I encourage everyone I work with to tune into themselves and their experiences to find their superpowers and build a meaningful and motivation vision for their future.

—Sheila, president and chief operating officer in
private education services, South Asian

STANDPOINT THEORY AND LEADERSHIP

American feminist theorist Sandra Harding coined standpoint theory while studying the epistemologies of women's knowledge. Harding noted that academic scholarship often is fueled by a "community of knowers" who are particularly homogenous—cisgender, heterosexual, white, and male.[1] She emphasized that although scientific methods and academic research are touted as objective, they are not so. They are infused with the standpoint of the researcher, and for homogenous research groups, one specific standpoint underpins the expertise and authority that establishes this community of knowers. Only certain groups determine most research questions. Only certain groups define the problem, pulling in data and evidence from past research that was also developed by these groups. And these same groups arrive at conclusions and recommendations that shape how we interpret the world and take action. This process creates a powerful, overlooked cycle of centering certain perspectives that are subtly subjective but framed in objectivism.

Within standpoint theory, however, Harding posits that those at the top of social hierarchies can oftentimes miss critical questions and insights due to their distance from the lived social realities of others. Living life at thirty-thousand feet does not give you a good idea of what is happening on the ground, more so if you ascended to that cruising altitude with few hardships attached to your identity. The power and privilege one carries shift how others perceive them and, as a result, shift how that individual perceives the world. As we have come to understand, perception becomes reality very easily, and that reality is then reflexively incorporated into research questions and analysis.

By contrast, due to their positionality, marginalized individuals can better pinpoint the questions that most need asking and explain the nature of complex problems. A multitude of different social realities take place simultaneously. If one is unaware of them, whether from lack of experience or exposure, their lens of understanding remains narrow and unacquainted with the nature of the world. Those who are marginalized or othered know that such marginalization is possible and therefore are more aware of when it may be happening to others, even when they are not experiencing it themselves. This is all the more reason why checking aspects of ourselves at

UNTAPPED VOICES

I would actually say that my superpower is hearing what's not being said. People who don't really have voices or don't feel like they have a voice, or maybe for other reasons like feeling imposter syndrome or identifying as an introvert and things like that. I'm able to because I know what it feels like to not have been heard before becoming a manager, and after becoming a manager and a leader, I'm more attuned and sensitive to whose voices aren't at the table. I'm constantly thinking about that space. That's really informed this leadership style, and it's allowed me to grow and be more successful as a leader because people on my team are feeling heard.

—Jenn, CEO of a diversity recruiting consulting firm, Black

the door when entering professional spaces can be detrimental for all. Our diverse life experiences give us perspectives from which an entire group can benefit and learn.

Although standpoint theory stems from the research of feminism in scientific studies and academia, the essential argument is resonant and aligned with leadership. We have a homogenous group of knowers that has created a traditional leadership narrative from their perspective, one informed by a longstanding privilege of being considered leaders just by virtue of certain identities. This community is particularly consequential because it informs organizations about what to look for in leaders and ultimately contributes to the disparities we witness in top positions and the inequitable workplace practices we hear about all too often. However, this perspective is limited due to the same societal status it has helped bolster. Those social contexts, which are very much a reality during and outside of business hours, are either completely missed or brushed aside for the sake of organizational outcomes. But is this the best, most impactful way to lead? It might be easier to dismiss the complex realities many of us face, but doing so prevents the definition of leadership from growing deeper, broader, and more effective. I question whether such an approach should be considered leadership in the first place.

To truly understand a system, you must examine it from its margins to its core. To truly understand the nature of a challenge, you must examine it from all angles, not just from above. You cannot merely assess what is visible; you must also consider what lurks beneath the surface historically and contextually. Based on what is already known, we purport to have all the information and know what to do, yet substantial important data is marginalized by default within our traditional structures. We don't include it in our decision making or our general awareness, so we mistakenly believe we are operating with a wide-angle lens when it is really a microscope.

With the evident gap in diversity among the leadership theorists, authors, and practitioners who can access the top echelons of leadership, the standpoint theory framework directly challenges where leadership authority lies. Leadership doesn't usually happen in isolated moments. There are exchanges between people, connections exercised, and group-impacting action taken. To understand leadership, you *must* understand people. Who better to understand people than marginalized populations, which experience nuanced realities of humanity while operating within structures that emphasize dominant cultures?

Understanding the deeply embedded narrowness of our scholarship and practice offers us the opportunity to explore the leadership standpoints we may be missing. Who has essential perspectives that we have not considered? Rather than look up to leadership, what if we look out and around? Or within? In a moment calling for our critical review, we have an opportunity to explore new approaches by widening the lens. A select few who are disconnected from the lived realities of the many can no longer define, hoard, and exercise leadership. We need to invite and value the leadership of the marginalized.

LEADERSHIP FROM THE (ASSIGNED) BOTTOM

Our habits and values have proven our commitment to a hierarchical definition of leadership. We equate the narrowest part of an organizational pyramid with "the leadership," disregarding anyone along the wider, lower rungs of the triangle. Leadership research and frameworks have been scapegoated into substantiating order and, perhaps purposefully, solidifying hierarchies birthed out of longstanding social constructs. When looking for leadership in top-down structures, we do not consider that assigned bottom tier. That is a grave oversight.

The easiest group to consider in this case are entry-level employees, individual contributors, or even lower- and mid-level managers, because our organizations are predominantly powered by those in these positions. Therein lies a wealth of perspectives often overlooked as our gaze typically drifts up the organizational chart when searching for leadership. This happens out of necessity—since the chart-toppers tend to hold the power that can most greatly impact everything and everyone else—and sheer habit. When in these roles, we often operate in a way that corresponds with what is expected, because not doing so could cost us our job. Questioning workplace practices or offering a dissenting idea from those in higher roles is tough because that is not expected of us in those scenarios. We can barely admit mistakes, even while learning a new job, without concern that it will harm our credibility and reputation. Thus, those who make up the base of hierarchical structures mute their perspectives to align with what is expected.

We miss a lot as organizations by not considering the perspectives at these levels. While in these roles, people often experience work challenges and unique opportunities up close. We use phrases like "having ears to the ground" or "being in the trenches" to signify the particularly useful perspective that can be offered from these positions. However, true inclusion often stops there. Those with positional authority might solicit these perspectives for their own interpretation and decision making, which supports leadership at the top rather than expanding the definition of leadership to include those most closely connected to the challenge.

I recall an influential moment in my own leadership journey when collaborating with an executive leader. I was a midlevel manager in career and leadership development for a top-tier engineering school, which was experiencing heightened pressure from students, parents, and stakeholders to prove adequate return on their very pricey tuition investment in the form of postgraduate employment. My role was central to managing this expectation since my office oversaw the connections and experiences that brought these employment opportunities to students, doing so with human capital that did not meet student demand. Given the power of the stakeholders involved, the

UNTAPPED VOICES

With my teams in operations, usually I have to get my hands in it so that I could get a sense of how things worked. My approach is "let me do it with you and then let's both collectively see how we can change our thoughts so that we can add improvements."

My approach is all about the engagement component. Everybody's input should be heard. That also allows them to see different perspectives so that they can come to conclusions on their own and feel as if they're a part of it. If I just come in and just say, "Hey, we're going to change this—boom," then all I'm going to do is disrupt. You have to first earn trust, and you do that by being in the game with them, not acting as if you are better than them.

—Noelle, vice president in health care, Black

challenge also required the attention of the school's executive team, primarily its executive vice dean, John O'Brien.

Given the nature of my position on the school's hierarchical chart, a step removed from the executive-level dean's office, I had limited interactions with John until this point. He was an engineer and professor who rose in the ranks and transitioned into executive administration, a role he held before I came on board. Based on some entrenched definitions of leadership that I still held at that point, I was admittedly anxious to engage in collaboration with the executive vice dean on this complex work challenge. I prepared copiously for our meeting, compiling data and summaries of the work and the nature of the challenge from my perspective. Although I was prepared, I knew that I would be deferential to anything John suggested because those are the lanes we create when engaging with leadership.

Apprehensively entering that conversation, my nervous concerns quickly dissipated due to the way that John approached the meeting. Almost immediately, he made it clear that he was interested in understanding the challenge from my perspective. He went as far as to explicitly state that I was the expert in this situation and that he was just learning to gauge how best he could support from his position. I was struck. With the power afforded by his title, John could have made directives, flexed his authority, or even feigned consideration of my perspective while ultimately holding tight to his own line of thinking. I've had my share of interactions with executives that have gone that route as well. Instead, I was approached by a leader who understood that my positionality—lower on the organizational chart but right in front of the challenge—was a critical perspective. Importantly, he did so explicitly by naming my role in the meeting as that of the expert, inherently acknowledging the power imbalance that formally existed but shifting it to encourage my authentic contribution. I spoke without hesitation, and he listened. It was a sixty-minute exchange that I've carried with me since as an example of leveraging leadership at all levels of an organization.

Similar to standpoint theory, those at the assigned bottom of a workplace hierarchy may have the best view for asking the critical questions that can move an organization through complex challenges and necessary innovations. The common assumption is that entry-level individuals and new hires need more time and experience in an organization before being able to lead, yet those individuals are best positioned to ask, "Why is this done this way?" and offer ideas for improving a process. With fresh eyes, they notice workplace procedures and culture that may be so embedded and inherited that others do not see or have come to accept their inherent absurdities or outdatedness. When getting acclimated to a new environment, we take stock of what is going on there. In our examination lies unique expertise that could inform improvements overall.

Imagine if, when someone new joins an organization, they are asked to share what has worked and not worked during their first months in the position, regardless of how big, small, or critical the observation is. Imagine what they might notice that someone else might have dismissed as "just how it is." Then imagine how much could improve because of that small exercise of being willing to consider the leadership of someone brand new, young, or professionally inexperienced. We often enter new positions resigned to thinking that we need to operate solely for the sake of our success, and in our current reality, that is very true. Just as we don't leave room for too many mistakes for new team members, we also don't expect much insight from them, particularly at entry levels. Team members in these positions might not be able to walk in and make consequential business decisions without more time and experience, but theirs is still a useful perspective—a

UNTAPPED VOICES

Starting out as line staff and moving up to the leadership team, I have found that the more power you're awarded, the lonelier the path. This was a surprise to me. I imagined other women taking me under their wing. In my case, I have found that those at the leadership level are doing way too much and don't have a free moment to mentor new leadership. New leadership gets tossed in with a sink-or-swim mentality. Also surprising is that leadership does not have any coaching or support for their role or wellness. They can lean on each other, but what happens when you don't align with your leadership team members? Where do you get to talk about this and work through it?

particular standpoint that should carry weight when moments of decision happen.

Looking for leadership should not be one-directional, only flowing upward from employee to supervisor or executive team. It should happen downward as well, from executive team and supervisor to direct reports and front-line staff. It should also be aimed toward entry-level team members experiencing a work system for the first time. In that unique moment, those team members can pick up on details that could otherwise be missed—like meeting inefficiencies, values that are misaligned with practice, detrimental office culture norms, and general practices that don't make sense. However, the likelihood that new staff would be encouraged to share what they notice is incredibly slim. Those in positions of authority or with more seniority don't necessarily want to hear that feedback. It challenges the system, and no one wants to deal with a challenging employee. We expect people to be easy to work with, collaborative, and positive team players, so we mute any information that does not align with what is expected, even if it would have strengthened the organization.

Dissent is not readily welcomed but even less so from those lower in the work hierarchy. It crosses an imaginary line, and we can guess who drew that line: those in positions we have equated with leadership. They set the rules of engagement and are unlikely to establish rules that risk their privilege. Those lines help fortify their position and create an impermeable distinction between what leadership traditionally is and is not. What is acceptable is explicitly and implicitly communicated in how we approach work generally and how we engage within work cultures specifically; simultaneously, what is not acceptable is also communicated. Predominantly white and male authority figures decide the rules of the game, both then and now, while those at the bottom of the organizational chart watch from the sidelines or wait in the locker room.

Broadening the idea of leadership from the bottom into more societal considerations, this could affect how we consider the quality of contributions from students, anyone young in age, anyone with a lower level of educational attainment, or any other marker that signals the stratification of leadership value. We often discount the perspectives of young people because, societally speaking, they occupy lower positions in the hierarchy. Experience from a certain age takes precedence (though given the way we marginalize older populations as well, that age does have a cap). We see this play out in school systems where adults determine what is best for students even as students say otherwise. We overlook the potential for those moving through the educational system to exercise their leadership capabilities mainly because we don't believe that they are capable, or if we do consider it, we very clearly distinguish it as *youth* leadership.

To fully understand how to run an organization effectively, it has to be examined from all angles, particularly by those new to it or from the structured bottom. True leadership should not substantiate hierarchical order; it should dismantle it for the sake of true progress and impact. Otherwise, we'll continue shoring up an antiquated model that does not cultivate the leadership cultures we need to tackle our many crises.

LEADERSHIP FROM THE OUTSIDE

By nature, systems are set up through interconnected webs of relationships. When we think of any type of system—whether an organization, an industry, or a sector—we are naming an entity that is connected to and affected by other components. By design, parts of a system ultimately create closed loops; unless they were defined and finite in some way, they would be

UNTAPPED VOICES

I firmly believe that those on the margins have the ultimate solutions. Showing this by calling in those most impacted and giving them space to articulate issues/solutions has been surprising to those in power. Those in charge often forget that the people they're serving have excellent ideas too.

Calling those to the table who are most impacted by a situation is often met with the notion that those in charge know better than those most impacted.

—Shikira, chief equity officer for a homeless services nonprofit, Black

difficult to classify as a system. As a result, it is important to examine what lies outside of that system or what is loosely connected to it through faint, dotted lines. In those spaces outside of the system, leadership is likely overlooked or discounted. We can look to the nonprofit sector to most clearly see how this plays out.

Because the nonprofit sector often serves as the safety net for the most marginalized in our society, its role is essential to the health of the country. However, nonprofit organizations are not devoid of the same deeply embedded traditional leadership structures we have uncovered thus far. In fact, in 2018, 87 percent of all executive directors and presidents were white, even though these organizations largely serve communities of color.[2] Nonprofit organizations, nonetheless, work on behalf of their target populations. Sometimes their decision making includes the perspectives of those they serve but not as often as one might think. When they do, there still remains an inherent expectation within organizations about how their perspectives should be expressed and ultimately incorporated. I have heard of homeless services organizations inviting those in the unhoused community to shape their work while also creating certain boundaries for engagement to ensure that their contributions are palatable to those within the organizational system. Sometimes inclusion is more of a performative exercise with an underlying understanding that those perspectives will be considered only to a certain extent. Even in the most well-intentioned systems, these solicited opinions have to fall within permissible bounds.

Harkening back to leader-member exchange theory, we organize our structures around in-groups and out-groups. In a way, that is the only way that systems make sense. A system has to be defined in a finite way that establishes its bounds, parameters, and functions. Some aspects are central to a system: decision-making bodies, funding sources, and those with the power to impact other areas of the system. There are elements that operate the system, connected by arms or spokes, making it churn and work toward its intended purpose. These can be departments, teams, role functions, partnerships, associations, and the like. And then there are portions that are affected by the system, be it customers, constituencies, or anything externally or indirectly influenced by a business's doings. Leadership is only sought from within the system's in-group, where the perceived knowledge is held. Those persons know best and are qualified to decide, wielding their influence over all other components of the system. When this work is carried out on behalf of those in an out-group, we have likely missed important leadership perspectives, even if those perspectives do not carry traditionally valued knowledge.

Traditional experience—that is, a combination of education and profession—is considered the hallmark of knowledge in our workplaces. When we hire a candidate, interview questions center around past work experience and education, which are used as indicators of aptitude for a particular position. What is often not considered is lived experience or other experiences outside of those traditional structures. Historically it has been assumed that not much connection exists between lived experience and an ability to succeed in a role. This assumption warrants testing, as I imagine that for many of you reading this, your lived experiences outside of school and work greatly inform who you are and how you operate.

The same is true for me: my strong work ethic is connected to the very personal story of my family's emigration from Cuba. I attribute my flexibility and ability to adapt to just about any environment to my multiple racial identities; I can flex and fit in almost anywhere. Growing up with my mom and maternal grandmother offers me a lens to understand how much women are capable of, informing the complexity of the load I am able to take on if necessary. Yet these core experiences are considered irrelevant to my existence within the workplace.

There is a clear distinction between life inside and outside of our systems. We create structural margins that are both tangible and evident but that subtly exclude certain elements of knowledge in professional spaces. We sometimes invite lived experiences to inform the work, as often occurs in social sector organizations, yet preference and even deference are still given to traditional knowledge and experience. If lived experience diverges significantly from what we value as knowledge, then that experience is devalued even more. In most sectors, such experience is not even considered.

The field of human-centered design, where companies create products and processes with the human "user" at the core, is moving beyond the typical user and starting to consider the "radical" user when designing. In

UNTAPPED VOICES

I don't think, as leaders, we talk enough to people about the history of the nonprofit sector and what our role is as a gatekeeper. If you are inside of an institution, you are a gatekeeper. Even if you look like the community, even if you grew up in the community, because you have been hired to represent the worldview of the institution, you're a gatekeeper. If you get to decide if somebody has or doesn't have information, programs, access, resources, or whatever, you're a gatekeeper.

If you do not face that head-on, then you never get to be accountable for how you show up, and you never get to be in question about who you're accountable to, ultimately. I think that really shapes how I look at leadership. If it's not working for them, then it's not working for me as a leader. My responsibility is to keep the community, and preferably those most impacted, at the center of anything that I want to do, recognizing that when we can center or design at the margins or pull folks into the center and we do that with clarity, then we have an opportunity to actually get in [the] right relationship around our leadership. Then we're not behaving in certain ways or not seeing things in certain ways that only center our own perspectives.

—Merle, CEO for a national nonprofit, Black

most cases, when we think of a population, no matter how wide or specific our consideration, we think of the "typical" members of that population, typically the broadest range of people who share commonalities in some form. Those who do not share those same commonalities are usually left out of that thought process, but they are no less a part of the population than anyone else. Human-centered design processes ask us to deliberately think about these people along with those who were automatically considered. This process requires a specific callout to ensure that no one is overlooked. Possible issues with the term "radical" is a discussion for another book, but the idea aligns with the need to consider people outside of our typical leadership systems. Those who lack commonalities with others hold an essential perspective purely because of that difference, even if the group is small in number. Their perspective represents a nuanced and more realistic understanding of the nature of the work, the organization, the vision, and anything else usually dominated by in-group perspectives. Oftentimes when designing processes or products with this out-group in mind, everyone else is included by default. Imagine if we looked to those "radical users" to lead—how different would our organizations be?

LEADERSHIP FROM THE MARGINS

Beyond structural systems that create certain parameters—walls even—traditional leadership structures also marginalize those with identities who do not align with white, cis-hetero, and male. They have been the in-group for centuries, and although there are increased efforts for diverse and inclusive workplaces, history has a long arm and that in-group maintains its position even today. There is a particularly powerful version of leadership that exists in these margins. Women, LGBTQ+ communities, and people of color are inside the system—they have the traditional educational and professional knowledge that is societally approved. They know how to navigate these systems and even succeed within them, achieving career milestones frequently despite existing barriers. They also have the essential view that standpoint theory emphasizes: due to their marginalized perspectives, they can craft more meaningful and poignant workplace research questions that get to the root of an issue. They often see the full picture because they

UNTAPPED VOICES

I think that the fact that I am an immigrant working with undocumented and immigrant families has allowed me to help them more and to be able to understand their struggles and how hard it is to sometimes accomplish a small goal and at the same time bring awareness of how undocumented families and documented families are different and have different difficulties, so we cannot ask or expect the same [from everyone] or even treat everyone the same.

—Patty, family programs assistant in social work, Latinx

experience and include what those who are centered avoid and omit. To a certain extent, they are the radical user.

As a result of leading through challenging work environments or navigating turbulent skies, marginalized leaders have toolkits equipped with more ingenuity and skill than those with traditional leadership profiles, and their approaches charter a smoother path to the top echelons of organizations. They tap into an undercurrent of a seldom-discussed reality that challenges the system, rendering it not fully acceptable to established leadership.

Leaders of color often navigate more complex terrain in their career course and therefore are equipped with inherent and unique expertise. Their standpoint yields a more layered understanding of critical work challenges and leadership approaches that are more connected to context than those with dominant perspectives who may not see (or simply choose to disregard) the whole picture. In many ways, marginalized leaders are in a better position to lead because their manufactured positionality in society has given them a nuanced perspective.

THE DISCOMFORT WITH SHIFTING FOCUS

At this point, I would bet that if you don't hold marginalized identities, you may have felt some resistance toward the idea of shifting where we look for leadership. Even if you do hold some traditionally decentered identities, you might also feel uncertainty. That is understandable—a change of this scope requires a great deal of unlearning and considering ways of leading that we haven't before. Apprehension is an understandable reaction because we don't really know what such a change means, what it looks like, or how we can put it into practice. It moves so far beyond what we have always experienced that a little wariness and hesitation is natural. In those instances of resistance, I encourage you to pause and explore the source of that friction just for a moment. What do you attribute it to? What makes you uncomfortable? Are there any elements of this conversation that may expose your personal connection to (and potential loss associated with) the benefits of traditional leadership interpretations—for example, status, financial benefits, security, autonomy, and so forth? Do you feel a perceived loss as the spotlight shifts in a new direction?

I pause here to ask these questions because they are all valid; you may have many others. Fundamentally shifting how we consider leadership should leave us with more questions than answers. In fact, after centuries of how-to guides and prescriptive definitions of leadership based on dominant perspectives, it is well past time that we pull back on answers and spend more time asking questions. We should come away with the realization that we have much more to learn and be open to shedding any antiquated models that do not value and benefit *everyone* who contributes to our systems.

Part II of *Untapped Leadership* dives deeper into the essential standpoint of marginalized professionals as a starting ground for departing from traditional notions and shifting to the leadership that is needed today.

PART II

THE CAPACITIES OF UNDERREPRESENTED LEADERS

5

STEALTH MODE

The emergence of stealth technology shifted the capability of military efforts in the mid-twentieth century. In the United States, this development gained speed during the Cold War in efforts to prevent radar tracking of warplanes. Also called "low observable technology," stealth machinery aims to operate undetected. A safety tactic that is useful in warfare, it also occurs in our natural environment, where different species use camouflage to hide from predators. Its usefulness and necessity have even brought about stealth bombers—huge airplanes that fly through the skies unnoticed. These machines typically have an outer layer of radar-absorbent material that deflects tracking signals and are engineered with an almost seamless angular design devoid of bumps or protruding elements. Their movements also produce minor frequencies that even the best counter-technology finds difficult to pick up. It is a combination of elements that allow very visible structures to disappear as if by magic.

Like "invisible" military planes that fly under the radar to minimize risk as they fulfill their mission, leaders of color adopt a stealth-like approach to achieve outcomes at work. Given the historical foundation of work, leadership, and professional culture, marginalized leaders must subdue or render invisible some aspects of who they are because the environment was not designed with their types of flight in mind. They often operate in imperceptible ways, unrecognized by the tenuous environments surrounding them. As much as we now tout diversity, equity, and inclusive initiatives, we are not flying in friendly skies. A layer of camouflage is still required to prevent being flagged as a foreign object in our own teams and organizations. We need to communicate to these systems that we are safe, we play in bounds, and we lead in the way that is traditionally expected, even when at our most authentic core, we know the limitations of those approaches. We reduce our risk by donning camouflage that makes us look and sound like the dominant environment. Yet underneath, we know it is a cover.

Unlike their white male counterparts, leaders of color require an advanced understanding of situational awareness, organizational dynamics, and sound decision making, given how significant a misstep can be to a marginalized leader's career. Our focus cannot simply be on the job itself;

UNTAPPED VOICES

A leader wants to feel like they belong too. They want to feel like they're accepted. When my team members let me know that I'm doing well for them, that I belong, that they belong, that we are working together, it's great.

There has not been a team where I've not had a detractor, however. I've had many detractors. They were very, very subtle. They were very hidden. They were very cutthroat. You never knew. I used to say, "I have to go to work and deal with the ghost," because you never knew who was in your corner or if they were ghosts. You couldn't put your hands on them. And when you tried to shine the light, they disappeared.

As a marginalized person, we're always on guard, anxious, nervous. . . . And then we hear others in the dominant group say, "I don't know what to say or what to do. What do you do when you make a mistake and you're nervous because you don't want to hurt any feelings?" I say, if I can be very candid and give you my personal experience, you do what I do every day. Keep plowing through. You keep moving forward, because every day that I show up in a group where there are people who can marginalize me, I am working through fear. I'm working through confusion. I'm working through anxiety and I've done it every day of my corporate life. And it is not easy.

—Janet, CEO in executive consulting, Black

we cloak our leadership in protective gear because only then can the work get done. Marginalized leaders often have the same objectives, key results, and performance indicators as their counterparts in the dominant group; however, the process of achieving those results is not the same. They do not have much room to move boldly in their work environment due to how their boldness might be perceived or even misinterpreted. The space gets even tighter when considering the societal realities that accompany them to the office and inform their experience there. Marginalized leaders have more than a century's worth of built-in stealth technology honed in the outside world and in a day-to-day work culture that traditionally prefers their presence to remain undetected.

Marginalized leadership activates stealth mode in the workplace in various ways. Trigger points call for added cover, particularly where someone is the first or the only person of color in a particular role or team. In those trigger points, radars that pick up unwelcome perspectives or behaviors are heightened. The spotlight is brighter, and the consequence is greater as leaders in this position statistically serve as the de facto representative for the entire marginalized group. Generally speaking, there are also constant and subtle calls for camouflage to operate within a system. As we have explored, systems develop themselves into closed, in-group structures to define and establish their purpose. These structures subtly scan the environment for anything outside of that definition because only certain language, behaviors, knowledge, and experience can validate that the system makes sense and can achieve its identified purpose. This type of scanning cultivates an environment in which people of color and those with other marginalized perspectives need to fly under the radar, because if a system is tested too boldly, it will extract anything that does not align with it.

Systems are designed to preserve themselves, and they work hard to do so. This is particularly evident in systems that disproportionally distribute power and leadership. In these cases, systemic preservation then becomes self-preservation and thereby a difficult entity to challenge. Because our systems stem from longstanding establishments often built with exclusion in mind, they become powerful structures. Marginalized leaders readily understand that systemic power and know that if they do anything that significantly diverges from the system's expectations, they will be spit out of the system entirely. It has happened and will continue to happen via

UNTAPPED VOICES

How do we make more fair and just organizations knowing that there's always going to be tension between the human being and the ever-persistent will of an institution to perpetuate and persist as an institution?

—Merle, CEO of a national nonprofit, Black

unwarranted work dismissals or limited opportunities for leaders of color who challenge too openly. And, as a result, many have learned to operate stealthily to remain in good standing for the sake of their livelihood and the chance to create change incrementally from the inside.

STEALTH AWARENESS

Leaders of color are all too familiar with the practice of scanning their environments, especially in professional spaces. With implicit and explicit bias informing a lot of interactions—and those biases unfavorable toward those with marginalized identities—the environment develops into one that must be navigated with caution. A misstep can create an outsized consequence. A wrong word can out someone as an "other." A misinterpreted tone can carry a long-lasting impression. There is a refined and advanced radar system in many professional environments that picks out what does not belong. So marginalized leaders fly stealthily in many respects.

Being able to navigate such environments requires a deep level of self- and situational awareness, which creates an additional ability to understand dynamics, groups, and expectations. Just like the planes that deflect signals to stay in the air and complete their missions, marginalized leaders subtly work to deflect any signs that suggest they don't belong. This plays out in a number of ways: through code-switching, tone and affect management, and even voice volume. Marginalized leaders are often calculating moves, not in a malicious way, but to help determine what steps to take during their workday and collaborations with others.

The result is a heightened awareness of one's interaction with the environment. When entering a meeting or any other workplace interaction, particularly for the first time, leaders of color often read the room automatically. Are there other people of color present? If so, how many? What are their roles and levels of authority? Who holds the formal and informal authority in the room? How are agenda items discussed? Who contributes? Who doesn't? Who makes decisions? This slew of internal questions helps leaders of color understand how to best interact with those in the room because every move they make matters greatly. Understanding group dynamics, especially if you are one of the few with a marginalized identity, is consequential to workplace success.

Operating with stealth awareness can play out in a number of ways. For example, an organization may espouse values of diversity, equity, and inclusion in theory, which do not necessarily play out in practice. Leaders of color often pick up on that difference very quickly. You can get a good sense of inclusion by how a meeting agenda is set, how members engage with those agenda items and with each other, and how decisions are made. It is not uncommon for companies with well-crafted diversity, equity, and inclusion statements to hold top-down, minimally engaging meetings or to discount or not credit the contributions of women and people of color. As

UNTAPPED VOICES

If a promotion means that I need to have access to you, but you're not comfortable with people who identify like me, then how do I get that promotion? Those things have sort of inhibited my growth along the way. You have to find these other ways of making it happen. No one wants to feel like they have to push into an exclusive network. Imagine how that feels. There are a lot of people that are strategically doing that. There are a lot of leaders of color in particular that this is a part of their strategy. They're doing things that don't feel comfortable or authentic or natural to them, not because it's something that they want to do, but because if they want to continue growing then they have to do it. It's so unfortunate that you're having to choose.

—Jenn, CEO in diversity recruiting consulting, Black

such dynamics play out, marginalized leaders take note and assess (and reassess) how to navigate their workplaces.

The ways in which leaders of color are denied power offer us a good understanding of who holds it. Through a lifetime of experiencing lopsided power structures, we often become attuned to picking up on power cues, both explicit and implicit. This may be revealed by who gets the most airtime in meetings or whose ideas are validated and implemented most often. It can also come through in what types of behavior are allowed and from whom. It might even emerge through what social groupings exist. Analyzing and understanding power is an important survival tactic because misunderstanding those dynamics could damage your career.

As explored in prior chapters, traditional leadership approaches cultivate a dominant leadership culture and, as a result, a dominant workplace culture. One can quickly pick up on what leadership behaviors are valued and how leadership is exercised in an organization. To do well at work, then, we all must align to those values and that culture to a large extent. Outliers find themselves facing issues of "fit," and course-corrective actions follow, often based solely on differences rooted in their marginalized identities. Confronting that reality is the baseline of operations for women and leaders of color in the workplace, activating stealth mode to align themselves with that dominant professional culture, even if that means performing in ways that feel unnatural or insignificant. Already feeling like outsiders, leaders of color work to fly under the radar and within bounds in order to remain in good standing within workplace cultures. Sometimes, it takes a bit more camouflage to achieve "fit." If the workplace is already designed for you to fit, then you may not have noticed your ease in that area or the difficulty others faced.

If you place a round peg in a round hole, the process is frictionless and almost unnoticeable. If you try to place a square peg in a round hole, the challenge is obvious and immediate. Marginalized leaders are often square pegs entering workplaces that were designed by round pegs for round pegs who historically ignored, overlooked, or did not want square pegs. Leaders of color might not constantly think about the historical context that informs work culture today, but we inherently understand the radar detection occurring as we work. This ongoing self- and situational awareness offers marginalized leaders a wide-lens view, which yields a breadth and depth of data that inform our decisions and uniquely equip us to act with nuance and thoughtful intentionality.

STEALTH DECISION MAKING

As leaders of color stealthily traverse various workplace dynamics and team structures, the moment arrives when they must take action. Connected closely to stealth awareness is a particular cognizance and process for decision making. Leaders often need to make decisions on a wide range of topics of varying scope and urgency. Overload in this area sometimes pushes people into decision fatigue; as the decisions pile up, their thinning available cognitive resources can erode their judgment over time. Given the need to avoid making mistakes, the weight of those decisions can get heavier and more consequential for leaders, particularly those working on a larger scale where decisions carry a broad impact.

Given how impactful decision making can be for a leader's career track record, reputation, and perceived abilities, leading with marginalized identities only compounds the load. Leaders of color face intersecting complexities, knowing that if they are the first, one of few, or the only one in their team or organization, then their decisions not only impact the moment and task at hand, but also can be viewed as representative of the rest of their identity group. Look at how the NBA responds to the decision making and performance of Black coaches, for example. It wasn't until 2022 that 50 percent of NBA head coach positions were filled by Black coaches[1] in a league where roughly 75 percent of its players are Black.[2] Decision-making ability in those top roles is not created equal, however. As a top Black executive called out in 2020, "One black guy gets a shot to hold a position, if he fails then the establishment looks at it and says black guys can't do that. White counterparts fail . . . all the time, and get replaced by more white guys."[3] Similar experiences have been reported in the NFL and arenas beyond professional sports. Organizations can heap added scrutiny upon the decisions of those who have been historically marginalized from leadership.

Leaders of color often operate under a microscope at work, where their decisions can serve as perceived exposure points that could prove those leaders may not be fit for the role. It's a subversive reality that requires cognizant and careful decision making. With the level of grace and space thinned for marginalized leaders, strategies to take action in stealth mode become essential. Although they may occupy roles of formal authority, marginalized leaders invest a good amount of their time and energy into building and maintaining their informal authority. They realize they need to build trust with others in order to be trusted to make decisions, whereas their counterparts whose identities align with dominant culture are often trusted automatically because they fit the traditional picture of a qualified leader.

In building trust and informal authority, leaders of color add cover to their decisions. When the right people are on board—especially if some of them happen to be at the top of the social hierarchy—then the leaders' actions may be better received, and they can accomplish a lot more. Marginalized leaders remain aware of this reality and incorporate these factors into their decision making. The traditional command-and-control, aggressive, singular decision-making style doesn't quite fly for these leaders, so they spend time building a cushion for their decisions to reduce the likelihood that their actions will be mistrusted and misinterpreted. They devote effort to cultivating buy-in so that others get behind the decisions they make.

It is important to note that although marginalized leaders' inclusive and cooperative decision-making approaches can be informed by the necessity of operating under some cover, it also is representative of forging through work from a marginalized standpoint. Leaders of color experience firsthand the detriment created by exclusion and uniquely understand the value of inclusion. Our decisions are wiser and more effective if they incorporate multiple perspectives and have been tested with confidantes and allies. Yet

UNTAPPED VOICES

My experience has been that both informal and formal leadership is centered on the ability to influence and shape the decision making of others to meet goals. While I have held formal leadership roles, I have found my informal leadership on issues and situations has been just as impactful if not more.

—Tammy, senior manager for an electric utility, Asian

UNTAPPED VOICES

Leadership is presence. Presence of mind, relationship, values. Leadership is a constant navigation, a constant shift and repositioning, to align mission/vision with decision making/action, intent with impact, and theory with practice.

—Sara, senior human relations specialist for
a nonprofit, South Asian and White

For me, one of the key components of being a good leader means sharing decision-making power with your team when possible. This creates a curious team that feels connected to the work they're doing, valued for their insights/contributions, and deepens our shared agency values.

—Stacy, family services director for homeless services, Black

so often in our traditional approaches to leadership, decisions are sanctioned only by the top and the few.

Although those in top positions are seldom able to fly wholly under the radar, some of their decisions are informed by subterranean thinking. They may favor solutions that seek to make the workplace more equitable and fairer for all. Even decisions about seemingly unrelated issues can serve an underlying purpose. It is not that marginalized leaders operate in deceptive ways—they demonstrate that making decisions to address the tasks at hand is only one part of the work. Acting on behalf of those following in our footsteps or other marginalized persons is the concurrent motivator for how decisions are made.

STEALTH CLEANUP

There exists this phenomenon that I call stealth cleanup. It is not uncommon for a leader of color to be brought in on the heels of a colossal failure of leadership, usually occurring with a leader who has been exercising leadership as traditionally defined and perceived. Those ousted from their top role could be let go after various accusations of workplace harassment, which is a sign of our reliance on undue and unchecked influence and power. Alternatively, when a business has been struggling for a while, a change in leadership is often the proffered solution. It is peculiar that leaders of color—women of color in particular—are given these chances to lead amid nearly impossible conditions.

I attribute this phenomenon to our inherent interest in finding new approaches and perspectives to lead. When something goes wrong, we identify the opposite of that something and bring it in. Thus, after seeing the harsh limitations of our traditional leadership frameworks through an individual's failure, we should seek out the skills and perspectives that will avoid those shortcomings. I cheer this phenomenon in theory because it sounds right. In practice, however, it plays out quite differently. Leaders of color walk into environments that are less conducive to success than before, inheriting the same unproductive cultures, attitudes, or performance issues. Yet they face the same herculean expectations that their predecessor—who likely had an easier time due to his nonmarginalized identity—could not meet.

In these cases, flying under the radar is close to impossible. In fact, given the external expectation to turn things around, such cleanup leaders probably have even more eyes on them. Yet most of those onlookers miss the strength and skill it takes to lead organizations in moments of disrepair while holding marginalized identities. The wherewithal required to operate against all odds is both difficult and deeply admirable. These leaders tap into their stealth awareness to deeply understand the environment so that they can redirect the ship. Even under increased pressure and expectation, they stay focused on their purpose and getting to the outcomes they were brought in to achieve.

Of course, this is incredibly hard! Organizations are complex, ever-changing entities during the best of times; during the worst of times, they are wildly difficult to drive. Coupled with limited space to make even small missteps, marginalized leaders are given less chance to succeed. And if they fail, the system is tricked into thinking that it should return to the traditional approaches that did not work before, without acknowledging the tumultuous environment in which these leaders tried to work. Their stealth efforts to steer the ship through impossible conditions are unnoted and unrecognized, even as these invitations to clean up organizational messes keep occurring.

STEALTH IMPACT

Aircrafts equipped with stealth technology often have critical missions requiring that level of cover. There is an essential purpose that renders the risk worthwhile. The same goes for marginalized leaders who stealthily navigate their workplaces and careers. Much of this is out of necessity, unfortunately, given social realities we are still trying to untangle from the exclusionary past. However, beyond necessity, a significant motivation is also a commitment to make a difference and have an impact at work.

Leaders of color often work double duty. They accept positions and contribute to their workplaces by completing assignments and delivering on the bullet points in their job descriptions. Concurrently, however, marginalized leaders are also working to make the path to success smoother for others. Leaders are acutely aware that they can be looked to as representative of any broader group with which they identify, and they carry that responsibility into most interactions and decisions during their careers. Their responsibilities are about so much more than just the job. They often prioritize

UNTAPPED VOICES

I have identified another more senior peer to share and collaborate thoughts ahead of presentations. We have formed our own leadership support team. Given our different roles and training, we bring different perspectives and skills but the same mission to achieve. She is also a BIPOC and a cis female manager leader. This relationship and partnership has been critical [during] both my best and not best moments of leadership. Her understanding (nonjudgmental listening to complaints) allows me to emerge from the worse situations to regroup and move forward with revisions, putting difficult relationships aside and being mission ready.

—Joy, registered dietitian manager for health care, Black

connecting with those who may have similar identities or who they have witnessed being othered. They may also invest time in mentoring those following in their footsteps by sharing more detailed and unfiltered advice about how to succeed. This work stays under the radar because it is often invisible, unrewarded, and unrelated to stated outcomes.

Knowing that professional environments can be tenuous, marginalized leaders work in creative ways to achieve outcomes. Not much is handed over easily, so trust, respect, credibility, and, ultimately, impact must be earned. In certain environments, those can be steep climbs. Numerous times through conversations and the survey responses offered for this book, leaders of color have noted that they prefer to lead from the back. Admittedly, it is my own preference as well. "From the back" may seem of lesser importance, but the origins of that interpretation lie in the problematic aspects of traditional frameworks. Rather than stepping out in front as is preferred in traditional leadership frameworks, marginalized leaders often do their work in collaboration with others, building relationships and trust as the primary approach to get the job done. And it works. These are essential leadership behaviors that move projects forward and contribute to organizational success. It goes unnoticed by those who look to the front of the boardroom for leadership, but it has an important impact nonetheless.

UNTAPPED VOICES

There's a phrase that has been told to me a few times in my career—"stay in your lane." That irks me like no tomorrow! In leadership and empowerment, there aren't any "lanes." Everyone and everything should be within bounds. In the times that I've been cognizant that someone is explicitly or implicitly asking me to stay in my lane, I've had the opportunity to inform them that is not my leadership style or what gains the best results. These moments of tension and suppression take a toll on me after a while, but I focus on the work at hand, focus on improving the team, and the community, and leap beyond that narrow-mindedness.

—Argelis, business owner in consulting, Latinx

In order to thrive, we must notice risks and opportunities within our environments. This cultivates an awareness critical to making decisions in ever-changing, competitive environments. We operate inclusively as a default because we know what it is like to be excluded. This mindset fosters workplaces that understand, embrace, and manage productive conflict as necessary in order to achieve meaningful innovation with equity at the core. Conflict is an inevitable part of our existence. We are diverse beings filled with paradoxes and lived experiences that can sometimes be at odds or at least drastically different from each other. Considering the ways it shows up in the workplace, we have an opportunity to manage that conflict productively toward meaningful progress. Unproductive conflict devolves into exchanges (or lack of exchanges) that erode personal trust and lose sight of or interest in a common goal or purpose. It's destructive, and it's hard to come back from. Alternatively, productive conflict embraces the paradoxes, acknowledging that multiple truths exist. It calls for us to wade through the disagreements to find the commonalities, even if small. It leans on optimism and potential rather than ill-fated outcomes. Individuals with marginalized identities, more often than not, experience unproductive conflict at some point in connection to who they are—whether that be an internal conflict in which outward experiences don't align with our perspective or an external conflict with others. It fuels our quest to have "real" conversations about diversity, equity, and inclusion at work, for example, knowing how difficult yet essential they would be.

BIPOC leaders develop an acute awareness of their work environments and keenly understand moments of opportunity and limitation. Traditional leadership perspectives often oversimplify the steps required for leading effectively through their airport reads and baited book titles. However, true leadership requires a stealthy dynamism not easily captured on a page. Marginalized leaders embody that dynamism, implementing strategies to determine when, how, and who to push when faced with a leadership challenge and when to pause, withdraw, regroup, and restrategize due to an almost innate assessment of workplace risks unique to people of color and other marginalized groups.

Our white male counterparts can often maneuver through workplaces with fewer repercussions for mistakes, eroding the need for deeper situational analysis of their impact. With their decisions and behaviors

UNTAPPED VOICES

I have often been described as leading from the back. What I have come to discover is that means I am not leading the way they have expected and I am not leading in a way that gets recognized or awarded. What feels unrecognized is that I am not leading from the back *and* I have no desire to lead from the front.
—Sara, senior human relations specialist for a nonprofit, South Asian

unchecked, they miss opportunities to enrich their leadership practice, which their marginalized counterparts do not.

WHAT THIS MEANS FOR YOU

The greatest source of innovation, critical thinking, and creativity results from people having the space to harness their unique viewpoints to bring both their best and worst ideas to a process. We tend to lean toward being polished, practiced, and boundaried when it comes to professional exchanges, often thinking twice before offering a new idea or a different perspective that is grounded in varied lived experiences. With an acute awareness of context, power dynamics, and culture (as not all workplaces may be conducive), why not say the thing that is on your mind during the next meeting or one-on-one with a supervisor? Why not contribute the thought that diverges from the group when the dominant line of thinking doesn't resonate for you?

To shift and expose the power that exists in the margins, we'll have to introduce those margins into the core of our work. Doing so may cause us to encounter headwinds, thus assessing the context is important, but these contributions are crucial enough to consider acting upon them. Change happens in micro-moments. Who knows? We might find that others hold similar thoughts. We might also find that some boundaries are self-imposed.

WHAT THIS MEANS FOR ORGANIZATIONS

There are structural and procedural strategies that organizations can deploy to create environments that are conducive to incorporating and valuing marginalized perspectives. During meetings, explore approaches that facilitate equity of voice rather than leaning on the person with the most formal authority or the one who is most comfortable interjecting often. Send out agendas in advance and request input or questions so that all have an opportunity to contribute. Include various modes of engagement. Discussion is undoubtedly an essential engagement tool, but couple it with exercises that ensure individual contribution, potentially in written form or through individual reflection, before jumping into dialogue. This allows time and space for all to put forth their best thinking. Set the expectation for dissent. Preemptively diffuse the heat of moments when disagreement occurs by framing it as a necessary part of your organization's innovation and impact. During instances when a marginalized perspective challenges the team or company, neutralize it by treating it as a gem of insight, no matter how difficult it is to

UNTAPPED VOICES

I am a woman and Puerto Rican working in a sector controlled by white men. I can lose everything in my career at any given moment. I know that I can lose it because those with power can, at any time and on any whim, take it away. And because I do not have the equivalent power and privilege of the predominately white, male powers in my business world, I exist in a posture of subservience that is neatly window-dressed as diversity. One wrong move—cross someone who is vindictive or don't display enough loyalty to a powerful person—and my career is toast. I get the signals and I see what happens to others who make these mistakes.

Being a Latine woman in my field is akin to walking in a minefield every day while trying to appear that I am steering a new (but not too flashy!) car on a freshly paved road. And the keys can be revoked at any time.

—Sylvia, CEO in biotechnology, Latinx

take in and even if you don't know what to do in the moment. This communicates to everyone that uncovering overlooked perspectives is essential, regardless of discomfort.

Cultivating a permeable and malleable work environment that minimizes the need for anyone to operate in stealth mode, of course, requires continued efforts. Months and events that celebrate diversity are one thing; instituting practices that value all facets of that diversity at all times is another. How can team members' personal values and culture inform the work, not vice versa? How can "culture fit" be fully influenced by the whole of a culture's participants, rather than imparted onto team members based on preset standards? There are no easy answers, but examining cultural, structural, and procedural rigidity may offer guidance into the practices that may be imperceptibly warding off marginalized approaches.

6

CONTORTION

When I was a young kid, the circus was a magical annual event. Seeing the giant red and yellow tent instantly conjured excitement and a sense of captivation. The awe, spectacle, and humor of a circus event sticks with you well into adulthood. I particularly enjoyed the acrobats and contortionists who seemed to defy all types of bodily convention, wowing the crowd by folding themselves into inconceivable shapes. None of it seemed possible, yet they bent and stretched beyond flexibility and into ways that appeared unnatural. They delighted the audience when they balanced on each other's toes, shoulders, and hands, creating human structures that not only required perfect balance but also a deep awareness of the other performers and of the overall risk of the act.

In the workplace, leaders of color often flex and contort in ways similar to the performers who impress crowds at the circus; however, a BIPOC leader's contortion is often unnoticed externally. To survive and thrive in the structures and hierarchies that have been established through a white-dominant lens, leaders of color must stretch in ways that are at times not natural. We have adopted work styles, mannerisms, processes, and language that often feel foreign, but we do so at work out of necessity. We have noticed which actions and approaches are rewarded in our organizations—with more pay, more authority, and more meaningful work—and we adjust and align our ways of operating accordingly. We avoid straying too far from those explicit and implicit norms because such deviations give rise to potential financial implications and career limitations. To align is to succeed, so we trade the professional costs for the personal toll of continuously self-editing over time.

There is an advanced mental calculus required to find the right balance between existing in alignment with who we are while also flexing enough to remain in good standing within a professional system. To bring our full selves to work would be a risk that could carry consequences, for our authentic, unedited presence reveals the truth of marginalized living to a well-established structure that is not ready to hear the feedback. Systems are designed to preserve themselves and they work hard to do so. The system requires those working within it to avoid diverging too far from its norms, otherwise, the system is challenged beyond its comfort. Many of the consequences that leaders of color experience if they bring too much of themselves to the office can bubble under the surface of workplace culture. They

UNTAPPED VOICES

I believe in leading from where you are and honoring the lived experiences and connections to the communities we serve. In my case, that means centering the voices of Latinx and immigrant communities. Senior leadership framed this attitude as "having a personal agenda" and not being a "team player," even when the mission of the organization was to support underserved communities. I was also told that I was "too self-confident."

They did recognize that I was good at building connections and expanding the organization's network of partners, and I was asked to train other staff on how to do that. They never understood that my success in building relationships lay in that same attitude that they were penalizing as a personal agenda, which meant engaging with others as my whole self, from my lived experience, and in a genuine way.

When I led teams, I was questioned for giving space to "junior staff" to lead components of a project. I was told, "Don't let them lead; you should lead." By saying that, senior leadership was questioning my leadership, and this critique was reflected in performance evaluations.

—Victoria, consultant in higher education, Latinx

often show themselves in indirect ways, such as exclusion from workgroups, limitations in responsibilities, or damaging feedback in performance reviews disguised as constructive communication. The out-group experience that leader-member exchange (LMX) theory describes starts to play out, except what is uncovered are the influences of the social hierarchies that LMX theory overlooked.

Leaders of color are workplace contortionists. By constantly assessing the risk of exhibiting authenticity and vulnerability in professional settings, effortlessly code-switching in workplace communication, and balancing the tricky and taxing line of tone, affect, and emotion management, marginalized leaders keenly understand what is required of them to remain in favor at work. They do this internal labor in real time while carrying the load of external labor expected of them in their roles, all the while others are completely unaware. If we are to truly study what leadership looks like—to understand how leadership can be exhibited beyond ways that have been traditionally defined—we must include and value these strategic behaviors and give them the weight they deserve.

AUTHENTICITY, VULNERABILITY, AND RISK

Authenticity and vulnerability have become increasingly popular frameworks for considering how to lead. It is a welcome shift from the more transactional, hierarchical, and prescriptive literature that typically overwhelms management bookshelves. The work of Brené Brown uses a human-centered focus to define leadership that is more connected to elements of the human condition that, in decades past, would be compartmentalized and excluded from the workplace. Brené's research explores the role of vulnerability in our lives, calling for more of it to be exercised to lead and live meaningfully. For marginalized leaders, however, the ask is bigger—they have much less room to bring their whole authentic and vulnerable selves to work.

In implicit and explicit ways, a workplace often communicates when there is room for authenticity. The concept of workplace authenticity bumps up against our notions of professionalism, which, of course, are practices that the dominant professional culture has established. As the body of white-led leadership theories and frameworks blanketed our interpretations

UNTAPPED VOICES

I feel like in the zeitgeist right now, there's so much discussion around empathetic leadership, human-centered leadership, vulnerability, and authenticity in the workplace. It sounds like the right thing. It sounds very sweet. But there's a part of me that's having allergic reactions to it because I feel like it's not really getting to the underlying corruptions, toxicity, inequities, injustices, racism, and biases that have percolated under the surface for centuries.

If we think of [leadership] as a physical entity, the structure is rotten and now we're putting on fresh paint. It's almost more dangerous and unsettling than old-school or antiquated leadership concepts that are very much grounded in the military.

—Sara, self-employed, strategic operations
and culture design, South Asian

of leadership in the workplace, we can safely assume that a particular culture of professionalism emerged in lockstep. The "how" of work was established by those with the power to shape the leadership narrative and thus informed only by their own perspectives and experience. For this reason, that culture expects us to "show up" to work only in ways that align with its dominant viewpoint.

We have a long history of disassociating our work lives from our personal lives, having been taught to check things at the door. The more we can compartmentalize our workdays from everything else, the more effectively and appropriately we can navigate our careers. Such a design most benefitted those unhindered by societal burdens rooted in marginalization due to race, gender, and other important but ostracized identities. If you didn't have to worry about how you would be treated based on the color of your skin or if you were not saddled with caregiving duties and outsized household expectations, then the luggage you checked at the professional door (if it even existed) was much lighter. It is through this unrealistic lens that "professionalism" was defined, and only very recently have we begun to shed the surface layers of that facade.

Given work culture's proximity to white-identified norms and the limited role of marginalized voices in creating the rules of engagement at work, the distance we must stretch to conform is notably farther. For example, Black women are 80 percent more likely than white women to change their hair from its natural state to fit in at the office.[1] It wasn't until 2019 that legislators introduced the CROWN Act to prevent discrimination against certain hairstyles that affected Black women most significantly. To change how one's hair looks just for the sake of fitting in with workplace expectations is the pinnacle of devaluing the authenticity of some. The necessity for legislation like the CROWN Act to exist in 2019 is our glaring hint that we have a long way to go before Black women and many other marginalized groups can truly engage in authentic leadership.

The spectrum of contortion extends from physically altering one's appearance to more subtle and unnoticed actions. This includes withholding certain cultural references, selecting more acceptable lunchtime food options, and adjusting word pronunciations and inflections in speech. It is a consistent and pervasive self-editing that overtakes our professional lives to such a broad extent that it often doesn't require conscious thought. It almost

UNTAPPED VOICES

What does professional look like? When I'm standing in front of audiences and groups, we'll have a huge conversation about professionalism. I'll say, "well, what about my locks isn't professional? What about my locks makes you believe that I can't deliver this work?" Really think about how crazy this idea is—that just because I chose to lock my hair, there's something less professional about me.

Let's really begin to think about this. Where did this idea of professionalism . . . come from? It came from those who were originally in the workplace. What you're saying to me is that specifically in the context of the United States, the more I identify as a cisgender, heterosexual, white male, the more professional I am, but the less I identify in that direction, the less professional I am. That's really what we're saying here. Let's call a thing, a thing.

—Jenn, CEO for a diversity recruiting consulting firm, Black becomes second nature, though not without long-term consequences: muting parts of ourselves simultaneously mutes contributions to our organizations. There is a proven cost to our overall well-being, as well.[2] Nonetheless, in a wide range of ways, marginalized leaders have engaged in this contortion to survive and thrive in professional cultures established by their counterparts who are centered in that same environment. If we were to reimagine trait theory, that subtle flexibility could be considered the ultimate example of openness, agreeableness, and creativity.

For people of color to truly lead authentically, that would have to include using their own values, approaches, and experiences, which would undoubtedly result in friction when they diverged from embedded norms. Marginalized leaders are astutely aware of the complexity of this challenge. They could use their own language and terms to describe the nature of problems and could move at the deliberate pace necessary to meaningfully resolve complexities. They have built the leadership capacity to infuse authenticity at work within the invisible boundaries that others may not even see, given that their version of authenticity is more readily accepted.

Leading with vulnerability is a significant paradigm shift from the leader-as-hero mentality we historically have held as a society. We are accustomed to the show-no-weakness approach to success. We expect our leaders to have all of the answers, to never buckle under pressure, and to avoid making mistakes. There is a certain sense that leaders are untouchable bastions of vision and guidance that we have come to value as a professional society. The ones who can handle anything are the ones who are placed at the helm of the ship. The concept of vulnerability conflicts with all of that. Recent shifts in leadership rhetoric have called for those who hold the most authority to show their cards a bit more. There is a letting go of the shield and a seemingly increased acceptance that leaders are human too. It is such a departure from the check-everything-at-the-door mentality.

This shift, however, is a much bigger ask for leaders of color. To shed the well-established and necessary armor we require in our roles puts the advances we've gained in jeopardy. Leading vulnerably adds weight to our uphill battle toward those top positions. It is a professional setup that leaders of color cannot afford to engage in, at least not until society at large acknowledges the lengths to which we systematically preserve a dominant professional and leadership culture that holds many of us back.

The challenge of leading with vulnerability is that first leaders must willingly share openly and honestly about their challenges and shortcomings. Then the exchange is out of their hands. It falls to how that information is perceived by others. Although this transparency could be an opportunity for trust building and support, it may not always lead to positive perceptions and outcomes. Teams that consider vulnerability inappropriate for the workplace could lose trust, disconnect, or hold on to traditional interpretations of professionalism. The exercise comes with risk, as leaders attempt to manage and predict the reception they might receive. That risk is greater for leaders of color, especially if they are the first or only person with a marginalized identity in that role or at that level who has been given the opportunity to drive. Because leaders of color also carry the unsolicited burden of representing a whole group of people, they operate under a different microscope with much less room to vulnerably admit faults or missteps.

The ultimate vulnerability for BIPOC leaders in the workplace is stepping out and naming microaggressions and inequities that they have experienced or witnessed at work. There can be real consequences for sharing the impact of problematic work practices and exchanges, ranging from having others dismiss those experiences as "miscommunications" to formal reprimands via poor performance review ratings for not being a "team player." Research indicates that to challenge a well-established system with difficult feedback—especially in regard to diversity, equity, and inclusion—is to run the risk of being relegated to an out-group or spit out of that system altogether in some cases. If we want our workplaces to grow in equity—if they are to take any action as a result of 2020's racial awakening and the virtue signaling that ensued—then these systems need to eliminate the risk associated with this exercise of vulnerability for leaders of color. Without addressing and alleviating that risk, we cannot ask those with marginalized identities to vulnerably lead with authenticity, and as a result, we will forgo their innovative, equitable, and visionary contributions to our organizations.

Leading as a person of color comes with an awareness of the many ways we can be misperceived based on biases and stereotypes that are deeply ingrained, pervasive, and persistent. To introduce vulnerability into this equation raises the stakes of potential detrimental impact if the risks are not acutely considered. Such an ask places us atop a tightrope in an uncomfortable position for dangerously too long. The narrative toward a more openly vulnerable workforce is a welcome shift in how we think about work. However, without naming and extricating the structurally embedded mindsets and environments that made vulnerability so difficult in the first place, the needle will move only moderately. If marginalized leaders can't access their vulnerability and authenticity, once again we've missed some cracks in the foundation that expose a leadership structure that is not sturdy enough for all.

A workplace devoid of true authenticity and vulnerability benefits only those whose identity, experiences, and perspectives are considered the norm. Existing in a society that has standardized your existence affords you added mental space to tackle the everyday, common challenges of work. If your authentic self doesn't test a well-established system, then you have the particular freedom that comes with being able to contribute fully to a workplace without much pushback. Leaders of color often do not have that privilege and therefore need to toe a line when it comes to openly engaging authentically or expressing any vulnerability. The heavy responsibility of being the "only" or the "first" in work environments is burdensome because of the unfair expectation of representing all others with similar identities. Despite this difficulty, we still find leaders of color who infuse their unique identities and perspectives into their work to the benefit of themselves and the entire system. Bozoma St. John, the highly regarded former chief marketing officer and first Black C-level executive at Netflix offers a compelling

UNTAPPED VOICES

Be present, bring your full authentic self, your passion, your love for others. It is all about you, me, we. We are all we have. Do not change the way you wear your hair, your clothes, the car you drive, where you live. Society will always find something wrong just because you are BILPOC [Black, Indigenous, Latinx, and people of color]. Believe and listen to the truth of a BILPOC person. For hundreds of years false narratives were written so that a certain population could attain wealth and stay in power. The shift of narrative to inclusion is real. There is no need to be terrified. There is enough power and wealth on earth for everyone.

—Kacey, manager in nonprofit community advocacy, Black

example of this. Bozoma, or "Boz," is known for leading authentically and unapologetically, which even resulted in her teaching a Harvard Business School workshop on authenticity, yet she also speaks openly about the fear and challenges that she's faced in doing so. Despite those challenges, however, Boz continues to have a storied marketing career by infusing who she is into all she accomplishes. Imagine the impact on the world if everyone could easily do the same.

CODE-SWITCHING

The balancing act continues in even more subtle and pervasive ways with the code-switching that marginalized leaders often engage in at work. A term with origins in linguistics, code-switching has become an essential component of leadership practice for people of color. As a survival tactic, people of color adjust their speech patterns, pronunciations, and inflections to mirror the dominant language styles at work. We use code-switching as a mechanism to assure those around us that we do belong and can effectively communicate in a way they will understand and with which they will feel familiar. It is a cognitive talent that is largely unrecognized. To be able to adjust our language in the moment requires mental scanners that assess the environment and respond in almost a blink. One can only imagine the impact if that astute responsiveness were redirected toward legitimate work challenges and opportunities rather than language management for the sake of culture alignment.

Code-switching can show up in many ways for leaders of color. It is the keen awareness that you cannot use the same phrases or accents at work as you would with family or friends. It could mean limiting cultural references and colloquialisms that do not align with dominant culture. Rather than saying "that's fly" to positively describe something, for example, we say "that's awesome" or something else that is more conversationally normative. It could mean leaning into more prevalent cultural references to build informal authority in a predominantly white workplace, even if those references are not of genuine interest to you. Ultimately, it communicates to the system that we are nonthreatening and compliant participants. It preserves a comfort zone that benefits those with power by keeping everything—even

UNTAPPED VOICES

Code-switching is a skill set that I can't put on my resume, but it should be a highly coveted skill. It goes beyond how I speak at work versus how I speak with my Black friends. It's also how you speak with one business partner versus another business partner. The ability to have that cognizance, that knowledge to flex when I speak to the CEO versus how I speak to the VP versus how I speak to a vendor versus how I speak to our Japanese partners. That's all a method of code-switching that people of color are experts at. This should be a highly coveted skill set for any leadership role because code-switching is very important. I don't know how we get this to show up on resumes, but I definitely think we need to figure out a way.

—Ibe, technical product manager in gaming, Black

the minutiae of communication—in line with their expectations. For leaders of color, it is a departure, a contortion, away from their language of comfort.

Although discussed as a necessary way of life for professionals of color, code-switching uncovers a unique cognitive ability that these leaders must hold, given that they constantly engage in this practice in the workplace. Code-switching has never been framed as a skill but merely something that occurs almost with a neutral interpretation. It goes beyond the typical shifts in language and behavior that can occur for most of us between our home and work lives. It is expanded editing that adjusts or omits cultural shorthand when necessary. Anything that is shed for the subtle purpose of aligning with dominant culture can be considered code-switching. Underneath code-switching, notably, exists a keen awareness of situations, environments, and people. Marginalized leaders can understand the recipients of their communication in an innate, nuanced way. Professional self-preservation is ultimately the reason for code-switching; reframed it also reveals an empathetic communication practice—speaking to others in the way they prefer to communicate.

The necessity to code-switch in white-dominant workplaces is an inexcusable element of our professional environments. Yet many leaders of color have this capacity to exercise language adjustments in real time. This

---

TAP IN

In what ways do you code-switch in professional settings? What level of effort does the practice demand of you? If it is effortless, how did it become so?

If the concept of code-switching doesn't resonate for you, in what ways may others be code-switching? How can you learn more about when and where the phenomenon occurs for colleagues?

---

cognitive flexibility exposes a leadership strength that, if given the opportunity to be redirected toward more meaningful uses, could respond quickly and effectively in various realms of communication at work. Marginalized leaders draw upon their intellectual resources when engaging in this practice yet are still capable of managing complex professional challenges nonetheless. What could it mean for our teams and organizations if those intellectual resources and that skill were put to better use?

MIRRORING

Extending a bit beyond code-switching is the concept of mirroring. It is an exercise that is just what it sounds like—mirroring the behaviors of those around you or those with power to remain in good standing. "Mirroring is a uniquely intrapersonal process that these employees undergo as they grapple with reflecting, mimicking, constructing, understanding, and portraying 'professional' workplace identities that simultaneously signal allegiance to their managers, defy negative stereotypes, respect the ethos of their cultures, and propel their careers."[3] It is a stealth mode practice. It not only requires a code-switch in language, but it calls for a code-switch in nonverbal behaviors as well.

In white dominant or minimally inclusive work environments, leaders of color mirror the behaviors of their environment to cultivate and communicate success in their role. They may adopt common language used, laugh along at jokes, and even adjust their preferred method of work to align with

UNTAPPED VOICES

I've learned to mirror the communication style of my bosses (who are usually white) to ensure that they don't feel threatened or uncomfortable. It's not healthy, but it has probably saved me some hostility.
—Bryce, public health specialist for a nonprofit, Black

those preferred by the team or supervisor. If the workplace is fast paced and outcomes driven, then these leaders mirror with fast-paced activity and an outcomes-driven focus, even if their innate preference is a process-driven approach that benefits from just a bit more time. If their identities carry biases of being too loud or too quiet, BIPOC leaders overcorrect or self-manage to prevent that bias from tainting others' impression of them.

On a recent family vacation, I had the seemingly fun idea to go into a mirror maze with my five-year-old. We were the only ones who wanted in on this fun; no one else was lining up to buy tickets. The teenager working the cashier stand assured me it would take about five to ten minutes to go through, so off we went. My son had a good time making faces into the mirrors that distorted our bodies, making us really short or really wide. We walked through the maze with our hands in front of us because we couldn't tell what was a mirror and what was an open passageway. We came across sections where we'd see our reflection extending for what seemed forever. We laughed and kept going and then ran into some dead ends—twice. The maze gradually became less fun. We made it to a point where we could see the teenager at the cashier's desk and the sunlight from outside but had no idea how to get there. My five-year-old became worried and, admittedly, so did I. I thought we'd have to embarrassingly yell for help. (We ultimately made it.)

Mirroring is a heavy task. Whereas code-switching can occur inadvertently at times for marginalized leaders, it is tougher to miss the ways in which we mirror our environments because they are more encompassing. Mirroring forces us to be conscious of our every move. These aren't mirrors that reflect our best light back to us. These are funhouse mirrors at a carnival; distorted realities through which we must find our way. The feeling is disorienting, limiting, and requires effort for us to find ourselves.

TAP IN

How often do we mirror the leadership that we experience externally rather than beacon what's within? Have your mirrors contributed to your success? In what ways have they inhibited your success?

TONE, AFFECT, AND EMOTION MANAGEMENT

In the permanent state of crisis in which our world seems to exist, a leader's emotional resilience increasingly has been named an essential attribute for success. Emotional resilience is one's ability to adapt and handle high-stress situations or environments. It involves strategies to internally self-manage oneself when faced with negative external experiences. Leadership undoubtedly requires us to steel ourselves against factors beyond our control and to navigate through competitive headwinds and unexpected downturns. Before our organizations and leaders were challenged during the COVID-19 pandemic, leaders of color had been building their emotional resilience as a necessary means of facing headwinds and barriers while traversing their careers. Even as the rhetoric surrounding this type of resilience has expanded, marginalized leaders have not received enough recognition for their mastery of emotional resilience.

Leaders of color must constantly manage their tone, facial expressions, and emotions to thrive at work. With a host of stereotypes and biases invisibly swarming around a work environment, any sign of emotion that deviates from positivity and contentment runs the risk of unfairly invoking negative stereotypes. It recalls trait theory, which looks for agreeableness, openness, and extraversion as a determinant of leadership success. Any misstep—even a misperception made by others—could have significant professional consequences.

Leaders of color are told that they are too aggressive, too loud, too quiet, too emotional, too intimidating, and too passionate (code for "too much") in professional settings, even if others exhibit some of the same behaviors. As a result, marginalized leaders remain acutely aware of how others may perceive their emotions and consequently mute and suppress them. It is an art to manage one's tone to avoid triggering a race-based consequence while addressing the challenges and conflict that predictably arise when people work together. It is an art to manage our natural affect and demeanor for the comfort of others. That practice is especially challenging when carrying the weight of the structural violence and oppression that affect our communities and circulate our worlds; despite the tacit request, we cannot leave such things at the door. Despite those realities, we have to adjust our facial expressions before the team video call to avoid "constructive" feedback from a supervisor. We can't reveal the host of difficult emotions we often experience at work because being perceived as a team player is necessary for advancement and pay increases.

It's a tall task for anyone to minimize elements of their human selves in any environment; to do that daily at work is an even more significant effort.

UNTAPPED VOICES

I feel what's unrecognized in the workplace is that leadership comes in many forms, but there's a dominant perception of what "leadership" style should look like for advancement in the company. I feel conformed to meet those expectations in order to be tapped for certain work or paths to success.

It's still a very male-dominated and traditional world. Even as we make commitments to diversity, the underlying current is still one that favors a system that was not built for outsiders or newcomers. There is still subtle pressure to conform to certain practices and styles of leadership to be regarded and viewed as a good and effective leader for the company. The "what" you do is more valued than the "how" you do your work.

I had a manager who gave me feedback on what I was lacking, how I spent my time with certain employees versus others and provided feedback on what I could have done better. They spent very little time developing what I was good at or even acknowledging what I value as a leader. On top of it, I witnessed new employees that did not fit the model were judged differently.

—Tammy, senior manager for an electric utility, Asian American

It can be argued that given our historical and present-day perceptions of leaders as ever-unfazed beings, many of us do this to some extent regardless of identity. The need for identity edits is deeper for leaders of color, however, and a direct challenge to the call for authenticity and vulnerability. The opportunity to be fully authentic is a professional luxury that leaders of color cannot typically access and an added layer of complexity and limitation in their career paths.

A NECESSARY REFRAME

At the circus, contortionists begin their routines by showcasing their unnatural flexibility, essentially a limb at a time, introducing their capabilities to the crowd. By the end of their performance, they have raised the stakes, usually folding into unimaginable forms while balancing atop a tower or a column of other contorted bodies. They have increased the risk and offered the audience proof of what they likely thought was not humanly possible. The audience audibly gasps, applauds, and marvels at the human potential they just witnessed.

The contortion that professionals of color engage in to lead their teams, manage their projects, close their deals, and raise their funds is akin to the grand finale of that circus routine. It is a high-stakes, complex, imperceptible endeavor that happens daily. Marginalized leaders exhibit the ultimate flexibility and adaptability, adjusting how they present themselves at work in big and small ways in order to succeed. They assess their environment with perspectives unique only to those who have experienced marginalization, accurately determining how and when to contribute authentically or take a vulnerable risk. They are able to align their communication style with what is commonly expected at work, minimizing cultural idioms or adopting common professional terms, sometimes not even noticing their own self-editing. Such a flex in communication style is an unnamed asset.

Unlike the contortionists at the circus, however, these leaders' efforts are unnoticed and uncelebrated even though they have resulted in unique leadership expertise that others should note. An understudied depth of perspective and awareness exists among those carrying marginalized identities in the workplace. Balancing who we are with what is expected is a delicate dance, and there is something to be learned about the leadership that takes place within that dance. We live in a world that requires a readiness for uncertainty. Contortion calls for a steadiness amid that uncertainty. The balance that marginalized leaders engage in almost effortlessly each day positions them to move their teams and organizations forward in the ways we need most. Our world also requires us to lead with equity at the core if we are to really have an impact. Diverse lived experiences inform the perspectives of those at the margins of dominant work culture, as those leaders have experienced firsthand which workplace practices cultivate inequity. Centering those marginalized experiences allows room for equitable environments to emerge and perpetuate.

Creativity, innovation, and impact exist in the uninhibited, unedited, and unfiltered contributions to our workforce. Marginalized leaders have not yet had the opportunity to contribute to our world at such a level, leaving us to wonder what we have missed out on. What answers will we continue to bypass while the fully authentic and vulnerable contributions of leaders of color are subtly muted and edited? These leaders are positioned to lead us into a more open, creative, and ultimately innovative workforce by nature of their full selves being excluded from authentic contribution. By folding in perspectives that have been overlooked, we have our best chance at uncovering solutions we haven't previously discovered. Leaders of color would not only contribute new ideas and ways of approaching our most persistent work challenges when given the space to do so, but they will also make room for others to do so as well.

WHAT THIS MEANS FOR YOU

As you consider how much of your true self you can be at work, take stock of how aligned your perspectives, communication and work styles, and appearance are with others in your organization. Throughout a workday or workweek, track when you feel most aligned with who you are, as well as moments when you don't. What is the context? With whom are you speaking? What is the outcome you are moving toward, through what process, and on what timeline? How do those outcomes and processes align with your preferences? Consider noting these reflections at the end of each day in an authenticity audit. We sometimes espouse values of authenticity, but unless we pay close attention, we may not notice the moments in which we're not fully exercising it.

There is an opportunity to raise your own awareness of moments and reasons for any self-editing that occurs throughout the day. It may tell you something about the source of the hesitation and offer insight into what steps to take as a result. If not much emerges as you audit your authenticity—if you feel you can naturally be yourself and are well-aligned and well-accepted in your work environment—then consider whether others feel the same. It may encourage a fruitful discussion with team members and direct reports and uncover ways in which everyone can feel more aligned and connected to the work.

WHAT THIS MEANS FOR ORGANIZATIONS

As companies and industries have spent recent months concerned about their "pipelines" of diverse talent and as we continue to collectively wonder why we still see homogeny at the top of organizational hierarchies, we should first look at the imbalanced way that these environments and structures interpret the contributions of their talent. We must look to the power that marginalized leaders have developed to effectively navigate their professional careers and provide them with the necessary space to lead.

Some aspects of organizational culture predate even its longest-tenured members. There are elements that we inherit, and we can't quite pinpoint their roots. Aspects of culture exist in both explicit and implicit ways. Embedded in that culture are an organization's explicit and implicit definitions of leadership.

Organizations must examine what leadership styles and behaviors are most valued and rewarded and what leadership may be going unrecognized. Organizational charts should not be interpreted as leadership maps, with the cluster of valued leadership behaviors sitting at the top. To begin to examine the potential in the margins, you must fully define what is at the core. As companies examine ways in which their interpretations of leadership may narrow within their culture, they'll build a better understanding of how to inclusively expand to invite and reward all authentic contribution to the work.

TAP IN

What would be needed in organizational environments to enable all team members to replace mirrors with windows? How can we create spaces where marginalized leaders don't feel a need to reflect leadership practices or behaviors that may not align?

What would need to change to make more complete, authentic selves visible and valued at work?

7

THE DECEIVING NARRATIVE OF IMPOSTER SYNDROME

Everyone has moments of self-doubt. We second-guess our choices or wonder if we have enough information to take that important job or make that move, especially if a lot rides on the decisions. Self-doubt is a normal but uncomfortable part of being human. It also carries an element of forced humility within it—we know we don't have all the answers and that makes us a little nervous.

These moments of self-doubt sometimes build into a much broader sense of inadequacy. We move beyond second-guessing our decisions into questioning our abilities and our overall selves, especially in work settings where certain expectations and evaluations can serve as markers of where we fall short. We worry that others will catch on that we not only are uncertain about individual decisions, but that we don't quite know what we're doing with our lives more generally. All the while, it seems like everyone else knows what they're doing (spoiler alert: they don't).

As personal uncertainty piles up, we move into imposter syndrome territory. Imposter syndrome as a term and identifiable condition emerged in the 1970s (then called imposter phenomenon) through research of high achieving women.[1] The original research claims that these women internally experienced "intellectual phoniness" even while achieving many external accomplishments. The phenomenon has gained traction in recent dialogue, exposing how resonant it is for many. In fact, it is estimated that 70 percent of people have experienced imposter syndrome at some point.[2] That is a huge number. With that many people experiencing this phenomenon, it begs the question, What is the cause? Statistically speaking, you are much more likely to experience these self-limiting thoughts when comparing yourself to others who are simultaneously having the same thoughts about you. And yet this keeps happening.

It is peculiar to think that we continue to study imposter syndrome without aiming to understand and address the environmental factors that contribute to such a common experience. Tackling the challenge on a personal level instead of a systemic one is a misdirection of focus for something that occurs so commonly among professionals. We should ask deeper questions: What is it about the way we have set up our work cultures that cultivates this sense of personal inadequacy? How have the expectations we

UNTAPPED VOICES

Imposter syndrome puts the issue fundamentally at the individual level. You have to shift your mindset, pull yourself up from your bootstraps, positively affirm yourself in the mirror seven hundred times, sprinkle glitter into the air, feel like a badass boss bitch, and magically your challenges will be solved. It doesn't factor in the systemic issues and what is happening in the environment external to the individual that would cause them to have those feelings.

Imposter syndrome also has a second dimension to it, which I don't hear discussed as much, which is that I think it's actually really healthy for people to have these feelings of doubt. A lot of the disasters we've experienced in recent history happened because overly confident individuals who were in charge didn't have any self-doubt when they should have.

When we just talk about the systemic piece of imposter syndrome, we're missing out on really understanding where these feelings are coming from for us and what they're signaling us toward. I believe they're signaling us toward community.

—Sara, self-employed, strategic operations
and culture design, South Asian

set up for performance and the consequences of failure contributed to the prevalence of imposter syndrome? Why are we so uncomfortable with not knowing everything? Why are our academic and career journeys riddled with moments of feeling like a fraud? What in our environments and our interactions cultivate such a feeling?

Until more recently, imposter syndrome has seemed to play out on a more internal, personal level, with many keeping these sentiments to themselves. But those experiencing imposter syndrome operate in plain sight, often delivering on work and achieving milestones while managing an internal dialogue that adds to their load. Rather than offer their best thinking and deepest skill capabilities at work, those of us who feel like imposters offer edited and slightly uncertain contributions. Note that work quality often doesn't suffer with imposter syndrome, because the response to its associated anxiety is additional preparation. However, we lose the depth or innovation that could have been achieved if the work was accompanied with confidence and self-assurance.

I have always loved learning. I loved school and have attended a lot of them. Although I loved learning, I admittedly never felt fully comfortable in the classroom. I could count on one hand the number of times I spoke up in class unprompted. There was no way I would *volunteer* to answer a question, and that resistance followed me all the way to graduate school. As I advanced, the fear of contributing my thoughts became almost debilitating. Even in discussion-based courses, I somehow snuck by without saying a word, committed to guarding myself. I worried that something I might say would expose me as an intellectual fraud who couldn't keep up with the rest of my peers—even with my grades showing otherwise.

What I didn't conceptualize until much later, near the end of my doctoral studies, was that I was experiencing imposter syndrome. I didn't trust my

TAP IN

Reflecting on your career, what moments have you felt inhibited by imposter syndrome, if ever? Shifting focus from self-perceived inadequacies, what might be some external factors that contributed to those feelings?

own capabilities in comparison to what I witnessed in others. I convinced myself that I wasn't as smart as my classmates and created the narrative that my ability to work hard enabled me to achieve my grades, not natural intellectual ability. I was temporarily relieved to learn that this experience had a name and that I wasn't alone in feeling this way. However, it also made me limit my analysis of this phenomenon to just me, as if it were something I needed to solely work on internally to overcome through confidence building and skill development.

Missing from my own narrative—and often missing in the dialogue about imposter syndrome more generally—was the deeper understanding of the source of the imposter feeling: the motivator that cultivated those thoughts. I recall becoming shy during high school, along the same time I began tracking for honors and advanced placement (AP) classes. My public high school in north San Diego County was large and diverse, with students of all backgrounds enrolled. That diversity didn't mirror in my AP courses, though. It was often me and one or two other Black students at most in those classes. The majority of Black and brown students at the school were in "regular" or remedial classes. Looking back, it seems peculiar that the school was awarded top accolades from California as a "distinguished school," despite evident but unaddressed racial disparity and without true academic access for all.

It was easy to notice that I was often the only student of color in my classes. At that age developmentally, though, I did not connect it to my hesitation to participate. I just became overcome with anxiety in those discussions and caved inward behind a wall. Conceptually, I didn't understand that these experiences were affecting my academic self-concept at a foundational level, which would inform future interactions in similar environments.

This imposter sentiment cemented itself during my collegiate career. I spent my undergraduate studies in the business school at the University of Southern California, a school in which you had to apply during your sophomore year, showing a certain GPA and pre-major coursework completion. I really enjoyed my major and fared well in the coursework even with the forced 2.75 GPA curve that the school instituted for all classes (quite a commitment to manufacturing competition). My only-ness was even more pronounced in those courses, however. I was almost always the only Black student in my classes. In fact, on commencement day, I observed only three of us graduating that year out of a class of *hundreds*. It was a stark realization seeing the student population together in that way without seeing many who looked like me. That disparity, of course, expanded to the faculty; very few of my professors were non-white. I shrunk in that academic environment, disappearing in a sea of very confident students in the racial majority.

These academic experiences set the foundation for the self-limiting beliefs that later extended into graduate school and ultimately into professional environments. During fundamental moments of identity development in those young adult years, I became very aware of how little I belonged, and that sensibility permeated how I moved through the world. I didn't want to call too much attention to myself because my differences brought enough attention. I wanted to remain unnoticed so I could remain safe, and as a result, I fulfilled my own prophecy by excluding myself before anyone else could. I did not see myself in these spaces, so I didn't think I was meant for those spaces.

Sharing this story today would elicit a lot of references to imposter syndrome. It could be lifted out of a textbook. But I cannot ignore the factors in my environment that subtly told me I *was* an imposter. Studies reporting the prevalence of imposter syndrome among high-achieving women and students of color use that term to place the issue at the feet of the individual. Rather than imposter syndrome, the feeling is more likely an effect of trying to thrive and succeed in unwelcoming or outright exclusionary systems. If you look around and find that you are "the only" in any way, not just race or gender, that reality automatically promotes self-questioning. An environment's design communicates that participants should look or act in a particular way. It does not necessarily require malintent by those participants, but it is a reality that impacts those who become prone to feeling like imposters.

That is the tricky thing about the narrative of imposter syndrome—it makes those who are already set up to second-guess themselves layer on more self-blame for their shortcomings. Like a magician deceiving an audience with an optical illusion, the narratives surrounding imposter syndrome create an illusion that distracts us from the actual situation and toward the easier-to-spot diversion—our own selves. Insult is added to injury by using the nomenclature of "syndrome." It positions the issue as a mental health deficit, framing that once again digs the hole deeper for those experiencing the effects of navigating challenging and dominant environments.

TAP IN

What if we were to reframe our definition of imposter syndrome as a natural response to environments where we don't see ourselves in top roles? Possibly it is cultivated by environments that expect us to perform in very particular ways?

How can we remove external factors that contribute to imposter syndrome in work environments?

Current narratives surrounding imposter syndrome place the onus of work on the individual. There is an entire arm of professional and leadership coaching devoted to supporting those experiencing imposter syndrome. A lot of money and time is spent addressing the symptoms of a deeper issue that is much bigger than the person seeking support.

IMPOSTER SYNDROME OR MARGINALIZATION?

The resident advice for those experiencing imposter syndrome centers on overcoming those feelings of inadequacy without the necessary interrogation of the systems that cultivate them. For marginalized leaders, imposter syndrome is much more than feeling inadequate—it is the process of a subtly exclusionary environment seeping into our self-perception of value at school, at work, and in life. Our sense of belonging starts wearing away with every microaggression experienced at work. The act of marginalization in and of itself communicates that "you are an imposter" because of your marginalized identities and perspectives.

I would hypothesize that there is some overlap between one's sense of belonging in an environment and one's sense of imposter syndrome in that same environment. If we all felt like we fully belonged—if we could bring our full selves into these spaces and could mess up without a huge reckoning in response—I wonder what would become of the imposter syndrome industry that has emerged. With people of color and women suffering from the detriments of our current systems, a lot of resources are spent on figuring out

UNTAPPED VOICES

I think we are, as people of color . . . trained into imposter syndrome in ways we don't realize. Going to college, I used to call it culture shock initially. There were things that I thought I could do well that I tried to play to my advantage in college at the beginning that did not work to my advantage at all. It was because I didn't have an understanding of how things worked differently. The idea of a "weed out" class and experiences like that challenge you. It challenges what you believe about yourself. Having those experiences over and over again in a predominantly white institution is the training that leads us to imposter syndrome.

It takes time to really push through it, but it still leaves its mark. Even though you graduate, a lot of those experiences that challenged you and challenged what you knew about yourself leave their mark. Then you go into the world and you try to think about whether or not you can do this.

—Tanya, clinical assistant professor in higher education, Black

how to navigate these spaces more easily. No one has calculated how much money marginalized leaders have spent on leadership and professional development in a quest to quell an imposter syndrome that is externally fueled. A financial equity issue is definitely being overlooked here.

The perception of having innate shortcomings crystallizes at work when we see leadership experts and those with positional authority who do not look like us. We don't have to be made to feel like an imposter through action; it can occur through mere observation only. White dominant leadership in organizations communicates a particular reality. Despite trying our best to fit in and regardless of how inclusive as a space might be, we may stick out like a sore thumb when no one else looks like us in the C-suite. Those observations of our environments permeate. They have an impact. With 70 percent of us experiencing imposter syndrome at some point, there are likely multiple causes, but for marginalized leaders, it is often a symptom of subtly exclusive systems rather than any shortcomings within ourselves.[3]

UNTAPPED VOICES

We all hear that representation matters. It matters so much because one of the issues around imposter syndrome is that if I don't see any of me, and if I've never been exposed to seeing people who identify like me in different spaces, it's hard for me to believe that this is for me and that I fit here.

—Jenn, CEO in diversity recruiting consulting, Black

Our worth is challenged when we receive messages from our environments that others' contributions are valued more. When this occurs, one unsurprisingly begins to feel like an imposter. This is compounded by the inability to make mistakes, baking in the need to second-guess decisions to avoid adverse consequences. The feelings that have been coined as imposter syndrome are likely a result of navigating careers in stealth mode, contorting through a funhouse of mirrors that distort our self-perception. Systemic flaws are being misinterpreted as individual-level challenges. We have been deceived into thinking that this "syndrome" is about us, when really it is about the environment within which we operate. With top leadership positions largely occupied by those in dominant groups coupled with leadership dialogue and rhetoric centering those same dominant voices, we easily see that everyone else has been left out.

What if imposter syndrome is merely our reaction to the difficulty of learning something new or doing something for the first time? What if imposter syndrome is our fear of making mistakes, given our history of unpleasant consequences, which have resulted from such errors? Since we are accustomed to placing leaders on pedestals and viewing them as untouchable and devoid of consequential failings, then it is no wonder we step into those leadership opportunities a bit more tepidly. What if we were to reframe imposter syndrome as what it actually may be—a natural response to an environment that only narrowly allows us to lead in very particular ways?

With our traditional definitions of leadership—leaders exhibiting certain dominant traits, serving as our heroes on pedestals, and afforded significant power—it is no wonder we recoil in inherent fear. We feel this when we interact with those who have been designated as leaders through their positional authority or influence. We can also experience this when we find ourselves in those leadership roles, knowing that one false move can cause us to tragically tumble down the mountain we have spent our careers climbing. It's nerve-wracking. It keeps us on edge at all times. It informs our decisions. It encourages self-limiting beliefs. And we mute our abilities in response.

WHAT THIS MEANS FOR YOU

Discussions about how to address imposter syndrome on an individual level abound. Therapists, coaches, and speakers aim to help those battling these beliefs navigate through them. Rhetoric has even gone as far as to spin imposter syndrome as a positive—a source of motivation to work harder and address our perceived shortcomings by learning more. That is an unfair framing and creates an added burden for those experiencing it. Once again, without acknowledgment of the systemic shortcomings that promote feelings of imposter syndrome, we are looking to individuals to take on the work.

Despite the troublesome rhetoric, some inherent aspects of imposter syndrome actually hold some utility. Imposter syndrome coincides with a propensity to second-guess and double-check. When feeling like an imposter, we work double time to ensure no one else thinks of us in the same way, putting in extra effort to prove that we belong. That extra effort is taxing and problematic, but when you ultimately disengage with imposter syndrome (as I hope you do) that extra effort leaves you with added skill and deeper knowledge when compared with someone who may not have exercised that added effort.

Imposter syndrome also creates a heightened sense of self-awareness. This awareness can unfortunately devolve into self-criticism, which can be detrimental to one's leadership, but those who have experienced imposter syndrome usually have a keen sense of their opportunities for growth. Self- and situational awareness are essential components of leadership, and imposter syndrome creates a practice ground for that. We become acutely aware of skill and knowledge gaps and work to fill them. Those who don't carry a sense of being an imposter may not be aware of any gaps, because they understand their skills and knowledge to be at the appropriate level to warrant their inclusion in a given space.

Having imposter syndrome implies an inner sense of humility. Believing you don't know it all or that you may not be wholly qualified likely means that you approach work with a humble attitude, that you recognize that there is always more you can learn. Though misappropriated by imposter syndrome, humility grants a particular lens through which to operate, beating out the unearned, overconfident, overbearing mindset that is unaware of the expertise and knowledge of others. None of us should move through the world as if we don't have more to learn or experience, and a balanced sense of humility is an asset that should not be overlooked.

Still, imposter syndrome is an absolute detriment to those experiencing it. It is an unwarranted coping response as a result of navigating challenging environments, particularly for people of color and women. To be very clear, it should not exist. However, for any of you familiar with it, I invite you to turn the whole concept on its head. The extra work you put into combating those sentiments with added skills, practice, and knowledge gives you an expanded toolkit that others who have not been motivated by imposter syndrome don't have. Embrace and celebrate the tools that imposter syndrome has forced us to develop, but forsake the idea that we don't belong or that having imposter syndrome is an asset.

A shift is necessary in how we conceptualize imposter syndrome. We can no longer suggest that our sense of inadequacies is a positive source of motivation to work harder and to be more intelligent. People of color and women should not have to shoulder the additional burden of repairing the damage caused by imposter syndrome while bearing the attendant load of marginalization. The phenomenon stymies impact and success because many are

UNTAPPED VOICES

Imposter syndrome was something I have had to—and consistently have to—address in my professional lane. Carving out space in white male-dominated spaces is exhausting but I consistently show up and try and am making headway.

—AJ, cofounder and executive director for a nonprofit, Black worrying about their own capabilities when they could be directing their concerns to work challenges or opportunities in front of them.

WHAT THIS MEANS FOR ORGANIZATIONS

Companies should prioritize employees bringing their best selves and their best work to their organizations. This idea of imposter syndrome inhibits that. Rather than the best, it brings dimmed ideas and quieted approaches. People and solutions fall short of their full potential. It may not be catastrophic, but it is preventable and therefore unnecessary. There should be concerted efforts to quell imposterism in the workplace, and it can be done. Of course, the best means of defusing imposter syndrome would be gender and racial parity in top leadership positions and diverse workplaces that include and value a range of perspectives. Efforts that cultivate authentic diversity at all levels of the organization also will result in many contributing more confidently in their careers. This is particularly the case for leaders of color who would experience work environments that are more welcoming to their marginalized perspectives.

Organizations also can take on the work in additional ways. Supervisory relationships and team meetings can encourage opportunities to admit moments of self-doubt or uncertainty. It can be a bit of a risk, but if led by those in positions of authority, such conversations can expose the commonality of self-doubt that exists within many of us. They normalize the feeling a bit more and create a system of support where there otherwise would have been an internal turmoil for one to navigate on their own.

Companies should thoughtfully examine how they create onboarding, feedback, and evaluation processes for team members, so there is a cushion for mistakes and the idea of a "steep learning curve" is balanced with a steep support curve. There is usually no time at which one feels more like an imposter than when first stepping into something—a new organization, a new role, a new collaboration, or a new project. Organizations can predict those imposter syndrome trigger points and build in buffers to support team members. This could include building support maps to outline who on staff can aid with what, explicitly dismantling the concept that everyone should know everything about their job, and setting up team-generated norms for engagement to build a sturdier container for the work. By instituting practices and processes that cultivate psychological safety, organizations can disrupt the propensity for the majority of their workforce to feel like frauds.

Although the work on imposter syndrome sits squarely with individuals experiencing it, the onus of the work must shift to those systems that cultivate this experience for marginalized leaders. Shifting that work uncovers the untapped capacities of marginalized leaders who are muted due to systemic barriers to psychological safety at work.

Companies are better off when no one feels like an imposter. Leaders of color are well-positioned to lead the way in naming how workplace systems cause and perpetuate this harmful phenomenon. Those experiencing imposter syndrome can pinpoint factors that contribute to it and lead us to solutions to reduce its pervasiveness.

8

LEADERSHIP PRIVILEGE AND THE POWER OF PURPOSE

In our study of modern leaders and how they approach their work, we can pinpoint certain privileges associated with leadership. Formal power might be the most visible, but informal influence is a related benefit as well. Then of course there are the material privileges attached to top positions and high levels of authority. When one's path to those privileges is smooth and expected, one has a different relationship with those privileges and sees them as part of the predicted course—if you do "x," then "y" will come. That relationship can render some of those privileges unnoticeable, less of a privilege, and more of "how it is."

On the other hand, a keen awareness of the rarity of such leadership opportunities for those with marginalized identities can shape our view when we find ourselves in positions of leadership. If your leadership trajectory was not paved by someone like you or if you took a more unpredictable path than others, then your relationship with those leadership privileges differs. Because we see so few of us in those top positions, the call to lead takes on added importance. We are less likely to take the opportunity for granted because we recognize the magnitude of the responsibility.

In this sometimes-uncharted path to leadership, leaders of color often orient themselves toward using their privilege for a purpose. Our professional objectives may ebb and flow, align and misalign throughout our lifetime, but we aim to hold some meaningful purpose within our work. We also often

UNTAPPED VOICES

I didn't even realize that, once I made the decision to become a manager, how many behind-closed-door conversations I would now have access to. I'm learning how leaders are making decisions and how many leaders aren't really as informed as you'd like to think. When I think of it as a privilege, I look at how I am using this privilege to not only open doors for others, but also shift mindsets about how the next generation needs to show up in order to still be respected and valued as a high performer.

Do I have to fall in line and deliver in the same way that everyone else falls in line and delivers? Isn't it enough that I deliver with quality in my own way? Isn't that the idea of diversity? Do not hire with diversity in mind and then tell everyone to assimilate. What are we doing here? Don't increase diversity, but then tell everyone you got to be a certain way.

—Jenn, CEO for diversity recruiting consulting, Black

hold the larger and broader goal of supporting and leading our communities. Understanding the vast impact of our positions on our specific organization and on our people as a whole informs our relationship to leadership and the power that comes with it. Untapped leaders carry within them the knowledge and residue of having less power in society, and that experience shapes how we use power when we do have it—we more likely become leaders of service rather than leaders of sovereignty.

ON PRIVILEGE

Given its nature, leaders of color know leadership is a fleeting privilege. Earning as a marginalized leader is difficult. Opportunities are not as forthcoming, as evidenced by the lack of parity in top authority roles across all organizations. At the other end, authority can be taken away easily. Consider the consequences when a misstep occurs or a leader of color is tasked to clean up an impossible mess. Leadership should not be bestowed on us because of societal positionality or unearned privilege. It is an ever-evolving practice we should work at and toward every day.

Diverting widely from the origins of great man theory, our approach to leadership has nothing to do with being a man, and being "great" is not required. The concept of leadership should be reassessed to include more accessible and realistic applications. Leadership can involve grand, sweeping, valiant actions, but it also manifests in the micro-decisions and moments of pause that instigate change. It requires deep self-awareness and consistently assessing our impact on those around us and their effect on us. It has nothing to do with the titles and accolades we have been awarded or the accomplishments commonly deemed worthy. As it guides our actions and decisions, true leadership is rooted in our responsibility to others, ourselves, and this world, rendering the need for status nonexistent.

Interpreting leadership in these ways is rarely included in the books on this topic. They tend to address how to lead instead of *defining* what leadership is. We should be asking ourselves, What is the purpose of exercising leadership? To what end do we lead? Why do we place so much emphasis and attention on figuring out how to do it? Fundamentally, leadership from overlooked perspectives rests on improving opportunities not just for ourselves but for our families, our communities, and broader society. Leading from the dominant viewpoint may include these concerns, but their importance to marginalized leaders is significant and consequential.

Leadership should not be taken for granted or siphoned off for individual pursuits but instead harnessed for collective success. BIPOC leaders often begin their work with the understanding that when the most marginalized of us win, we all win. Those whose experiences are normally centered lose nothing when others win; more experiences are merely added. This inclusive understanding informs the way leaders of color lead. We know

UNTAPPED VOICES

My leading is making sure that there is a "we," and the "we" has power to achieve and to change.
—Sara, senior human relations specialist for a nonprofit, South Asian

the benefits of collective success because we exercise it in our communities and because we have experienced the alternative—individual success that often occurs on the backs of the collective contribution. For these reasons, we adopt a more connected and more communal approach to leadership, appropriating its power and privilege in an effective, equitable way.

ON PURPOSE

Finding our purpose is a consistent component of our career journey. On paper, we assume this purpose finds us in college: we choose our course of study, commit to a career trajectory, and set out on our purposeful path. Such an outlined experience is rare, for the reality of finding your purpose is much less linear. Many spend a lifetime searching for it with varying success. From a very young age, we receive different messages about our natural abilities or the roles we could fulfill in adulthood, often phrased as, "What do you want to be when you grow up?" which interlocks identity with profession. Depending largely on our level of access, we experience a range of exposure to these future possibilities. We can spend years, even decades, decoding our career paths trying to clarify what we actually want versus what others have wanted from and for us.

Purpose plays a significant role in the human experience. We want to feel like our limited time on earth is not spent in vain, that we somehow left a meaningful mark, whether big or small. Having a purpose also feels good. It offers us a sense of direction, especially when navigating tumultuous or unfamiliar terrain. It motivates and provides the energy to persevere because we understand the point of the undertaking. It also gives us clarity to set a course or backtrack to one we inadvertently abandoned. Amid chaos and uncertainty, it can quiet the noise and help steady our souls. With so much richness to offer, it is no wonder we are always on a quest to find our purpose.

Defining your purpose beyond your career is essential for sustainability and fulfillment. We tend to center our purpose within our profession, which is understandable but limiting, resulting in confusion, disillusionment, or worse when our work experiences fall short of expectations. We might feel "off purpose," which is likely a symptom of a career misalignment of some

UNTAPPED VOICES

There's a quote from Antoine de Saint-Exupéry that says "If you want to build a ship, don't drum up the people to gather wood, divide the work, and give orders. Instead, teach them to yearn for the vast and endless sea." If you can also help people reach their objectives and figure out a way to tie it into the greater good, that's being a capable leader.

—Ibe, technical product manager in gaming, Black

other kind. Because we tend to weigh professional purpose heavily, when our professional realities fall short due to external factors such as limited opportunities and challenging work cultures, we can lose motivation, direction, and satisfaction. Broadening our concept of purpose creates a deeper container in which we can include a profession, personal goals, and other components of a meaningful life.

There is a breadth of cultures and traditions within marginalized communities that serves to shape their members and connect them together. Certain hardships and challenges can accompany those marginalized identities, forming an undercurrent of commonality beneath their unique sense of community. For leaders of color, the definition of "community" includes those with whom they identify and commonly extend to those with whom they don't. No group is a monolith, and lumping distinct individuals together into a defined group creates its own problematic consequences. But based on how others interact with and interpret those particular groups, some personal experiences can expand into a collective one. As a result, we build unique and deep connections with others with whom we identify and, by nature of experiencing marginalization, we build a community-minded lens when considering our impact.

Marginalized leaders are constantly losing out on leadership opportunities, so they intimately know the impact of everyone winning. Inclusion is almost always a central component of their purpose, whether stated or not. Holding the unique vantage point of exclusion, BIPOC leaders, no matter how they identify, operate with a concurrent purpose to benefit their societal

UNTAPPED VOICES

The values that have guided me were always approaching work and life with curiosity and respect for others, acting from a growth mindset, constantly reflecting on lessons learned, centering personal and collective values, doing work that is meaningful in partnership with others, engaging in relationship building, always being transparent, and a lot of perseverance.

—Victoria, research and evaluation consultant
for higher education, Latinx

community and their professional environments. This work shows up in many ways. Leaders may leverage their stealth impact to mentor others with whom they identify and who are following their path, imparting some of the unsaid rules for engagement required for success. In meetings or projects,

UNTAPPED VOICES

Serving unhoused singles and families is *fast* work. The folks we serve have lives that change on a dime, which requires the provider to quickly pivot. Although this pivot is fast moving, it also requires slowing down, a chance to ask good questions that help to reveal all the layers of the fast-moving situation. The slowing down is counter to what the social work industry pushes. The industry pushes for fast assessments by skipping the slower work of getting to know the person's history/background/contributing factors. When wanting to lean into the slower work, there is always pushback. The pushback says, "move faster"; "make a diagnosis so we can move to treatment/ close the case"; "make your best guess and put that in the report." The intersectional work always requires looking at culture, racism, anti-Blackness. When weaving in these "taboo" layers, a lot of the pushback is "You're overcomplicating matters."

—Shikira, chief equity officer for homeless services, Black

they may speak up when something excludes particular perspectives or might be inequitable in nature. They may consider the ways that their positional or financial power can benefit their communities. It is not enough to just get the job done—they want to continually improve the professional reality for others with a similar career trajectory.

Leading with a broader purpose is a complex endeavor. Sometimes it runs counter to what is expected or requires different pacing than what an organization is accustomed to. Incorporating that larger purpose into competing priorities can be challenging, especially when others are unaware or otherwise ignorant of that effort. Similar to operating in stealth mode, marginalized leaders can carry an additional mental and emotional load while executing their goal to create more equitable, fair, and representative workplaces in the ways in which they are able.

WHAT THIS MEANS FOR YOU

We have an opportunity to think about leadership holistically as we consider why we lead. How do you define leadership outside of professional work? What calls you to lead and for what purpose? Consider engaging in reflection that takes into account *all* aspects of who you are and your many roles. What part does family play? Friends? Other connections? What do you want to experience in this lifetime, and how does that goal inform your work? What are the ways in which the broader realities of our society—its policies and power structures—could improve, and what can you do to support those improvements?

If we consider the privilege we hold when given the opportunity to lead as a task larger than ourselves, it starts to inform the way we make decisions. To shift our prospective impact, we can ask ourselves, "Are the ways I am leading and the decisions I am making benefiting others, particularly the most marginalized?" We can move away from any self-preserving and self-serving aspects of leadership that often emerge in traditional structures and move toward a realization that it's not about us—or not *just* about us.

Generally, we tend to orient toward the bottom line—the visible outcomes, benchmarks, key progress indicators, objectives and key results, email inboxes, to-do lists, and the like—because they prove progress and

UNTAPPED VOICES

Leadership is an investment in the people. That's not how my current organization thinks of leadership. Leadership here is essentially getting things done. It's checking boxes. The fact that I spend time investing in my team I don't think is valued within the culture.

—Nico, managing director for a national nonprofit, Black

performance. Those metrics play an important role, but they are not everything. We need to become comfortable with thinking about and putting energy toward the intangibles. How can you leverage the power and influence typically tied to leadership to create broad societal impact beyond the bottom line? If you are leading in a role without positional authority, how can your larger purpose inform your individual contributions to teams or projects?

Thinking about your purpose outside of professional titles can be a profound exercise. During a leadership storytelling session for women of color I co-facilitated with BIPOC political consultant Holly Lim, she asked, "Who are you when not considering all your roles?" When you name your purpose outside of your positions or roles, it allows you to work from within, from what is inherent, versus from without, or from what your expected purpose is. How can you access more expanded definitions of purpose that center on collective well-being and success? If we are not considering purpose in this way, then what is our work all for?

As a leader, you have a responsibility to consider the privilege of your position. It is not something to take for granted but instead to exercise for the greater good. Impactful leadership moves beyond the task or responsibilities at hand and requires a deeper connection to others, communities, and society. It should not occur in a vacuum and get lost in the day-to-day trivialities of the work. Reflecting on your unique role in creating the world we want to see is an essential exercise in embodying authentic leadership.

WHAT THIS MEANS FOR ORGANIZATIONS

Understanding team members' purpose and values should be a fundamental component of the onboarding, supervision, and teamwork process. Organizations should shed the "check your baggage at the door" mentality inherent to our work culture because our broader purpose and the personal fuel propelling us to work can also get checked there as well. We turn our "work selves" on while dimming the glow of our personal selves, and companies benefit most when all the lights are on.

There is likely some friction between current practices and culture and the quest to invite a more nuanced and complex purpose into the workplace. This tension can result in challenging conversations or critical feedback about how organizations inhibit progress in this area. Given our traditional approaches to work, it is easier to focus expectations on the organization's overall mission or the demands of individual roles. Mentoring others or naming inequities can remain unseen or be discouraged easily because they have gone unaddressed for so long.

Companies can work to remove barriers that inhibit their employees' abilities to exercise their larger purpose. Create onboarding processes that invite team members and supervisors alike to share their purpose and values. An employee's introduction to a new company and position should be learning about the scope of their responsibilities and learning about the people with whom they'll be doing that work.

In discussing purpose with teams and organizations, I have seen how few companies have created mechanisms for staff to share and connect with each other's purpose. Sharing that larger purpose and where it stemmed from—usually outside their professional work—allowed teams who had worked together for years to learn something new and fundamental about what drives and fulfills their colleagues. Equipped with this deeper understanding, teams built the capacity to incorporate those purposes and perspectives more readily in the day-to-day. Trust and relationships naturally deepened as people got to know fuller versions of their teammates. On diverse teams, in particular, the invitation to share one's larger purpose cultivates a nuanced and layered work environment that soon defaults to inclusion and a more accurate understanding of the ways that team members can contribute different perspectives to a shared goal.

UNTAPPED VOICES

Growing up in Vietnam, it's a very community-based culture. Being a part of that community really also helped define leadership for me. It doesn't have to be work related.

Growing up was a lot about giving back to society and others in the community. That really helps define a lot of my career. I want to be able to be part of a company and in a certain role that will help customers. But also, I want to be in a role where I can help and empower a team or work where I can help add value. To me, I get energy out of it. It's very satisfying to see the value that I add, but also the impact that I have on the people that I work with or work for.

—Ly, chief strategy and growth officer for consumer products, Asian

9

THE INEQUITABLE LEADERSHIP LOAD

Many of us remember where we were and what we were doing when we heard there was a video circulating of a Black man dying under the knee of a cop in Minneapolis, Minnesota. I recall that just a few weeks earlier, I had gone on a jog on May 8, 2020, in honor of the birthday of Ahmaud Arbery, the Black man who was out for a run and killed by two white men in a racially motivated crime. I remember the emotion of that run, thinking about the twenty-five-year-old who was likely enjoying a moment of exercise and scenery in his neighborhood as I often have in my own neighborhood.

It was a heavy time, as details concurrently emerged surrounding the killing of Breonna Taylor, who was sleeping in her home when police entered and riddled the apartment with bullets. It is particularly tough to think of someone dying by gunfire while resting. We all want and deserve safety and comfort in our own homes, so the details of the case and the subsequent trial results were difficult to swallow.

Into this context came the gruesome details of George Floyd's murder on May 25, 2020, which was captured on video. I had no interest in watching the video and the virality of violence but acknowledge the role it played in igniting a massive Black Lives Matter movement across the world. Seeing the images and reading about the pleas that George Floyd gasped with his final breaths hit the core of my being. How could something like this even be possible? It was simultaneously enraging and depressing.

Although not on the same level of tragedy, thankfully, on the same day that George Floyd was murdered, a viral video emerged of a white woman in Central Park calling the police on a bird-watching Black man who simply asked her to leash her dog as required by the policies of the park. That video I did watch, and it was incredibly troubling to witness. The woman yelled aggressively at the man, who, given her unnecessary intensity, recorded the exchange on his phone. Once the woman got the police on the phone, there was a perceptible shift in her tone, communicating that she was in danger. Those of us who are Black or identify as a person of color knew exactly what she was doing—playing into the reality that a police officer would believe her story more readily than his because he is Black. With Black people being 2.9 times more likely to be killed by police than white people, that call carried added danger.[1]

UNWANTED SOCIETAL BAGGAGE

The challenging reality for Black and brown leaders is that we must show up to lead while also witnessing our communities, loved ones, and ourselves as the targets of systemic violence. It is a heavy and often invisible load in professional environments. The world seemed to wake up after watching George Floyd, but many of us wondered what took so long and why it required such disturbing footage for that racial awakening to happen; George Floyd was not the first Black person to die unnecessarily in such a way. Nonetheless, we show up to meetings and deliver projects often without a misstep on the heels of countless other deaths fueled by racial bias. Thus our leadership reality is much different than what is painted in the many leadership how-to books out there. The lists and the prescriptive how-tos fall flat for leaders of color who internalize images of racial violence as they get dressed for the day and check their work calendars.

Entering professional environments while these awful news updates continue to pour in is an incredibly challenging experience. Prior to George Floyd, it was a silent undertaking for the most part, left to personal management and coping, as the work continued without skipping a beat. Before George Floyd, much of this violence wouldn't even be acknowledged or mentioned. The expectation of compartmentalization was particularly high, whether that lack of acknowledgment was purposeful, management deeming those discussions inappropriate in professional settings, or inadvertent, with many unaware of the toll this troubling reality exacted on some communities. For those navigating predominantly white workplaces or industries, the silence was deafening and detrimental. Couple this with the fact that if you were Black, Hispanic, or American Indian/Alaska Native, you were twice as likely to have someone in your family or community die from COVID-19

UNTAPPED VOICES

We sit back and watch these traumas happen to our community and then we're still expected to be on the Zoom call. After the shooting in Buffalo and then the shooting at the school, I woke up that next morning and I thought to myself, "Damn, I don't even know what to say. I'm out of words. I'm out of words of what to say again and again and again." And I don't want to continue with "thoughts and prayers." But, as the chair of the DEI [diversity, equity, and inclusion] council, as a parent, I'm out of freaking words. I don't know what to say.

I think what's hard is that you're navigating all of that as a leader. As a woman, as a leader, as a woman of color, I'm trying to make sure that I'm giving fair time to everything that happens. Even though every time when it's something in my community, it literally feels like a gut punch or literally someone has hit me in my face.

I would say prior to George Floyd's murder I very much struggled with showing vulnerability as a leader. Since then, I don't care. You need to know what the deal is. And that was what I said to some of the senior leaders after George Floyd's death. As we were talking about, "What do we do? What do we say?" I said, "You're horrified only because you've *seen* this." I said, "From my community, it's Tuesday, meaning we've seen this again and again and again. It's Tuesday. It just happened to get filmed. This has been happening for four hundred years. It's not new."

That's what I think is hard is that you have to navigate all of that. How do you give it fair time? How do you be a leader and how do you demonstrate the vulnerability and the leadership?

—Carole, director of marketing for a staffing
and recruitment firm, Black

due to the stark racial disparities that were uncovered as a result of the virus.[2] It is hard to imagine working at full capacity and capability while carrying such an overwhelming societal reality on our shoulders.

INVISIBLE LABOR

It may have been the COVID-19 pandemic that forced the world to pause or slow its constant cycle of activity and productivity and notice George Floyd's awful death. I recall how wild it was to see so many companies release statements and pledges voicing support for Black Lives Matter and to witness the number of friends and acquaintances rushing to educate themselves on the issues. It was a lot to take in. Although a welcome shift in concern and attention, it was unnerving to witness how shielded many colleagues and coworkers were, given their shocked response to this new awareness. We also soon uncovered which statements were performative and how organizations leaned on the added, often unpaid, labor of their employees of color to lead reactive efforts for diversity, equity, and inclusion.

Suddenly, since 2020, leaders of color have been navigating new and unexpected waters at work as well as the added complexity of operating in an increasingly virtual world. After years of flying in stealth mode, aiming to remain unnoticed as an "other" in the workplace, the spotlight has suddenly shifted but not always for the best. Companies energetically called for racial equity. Many were well meaning, some were virtue signaling, following the tide of the time, but few instituted substantial structural changes to achieve that equity. Most common was the creation of committees, task forces, initiatives, and surveys that looked to employees, particularly those of color, to divulge their assessment of culture, access, and opportunity within their organizations. Implicit bias training became standard, and staff retreats to poke and stir centuries-entrenched dynamics were instituted with hopes of some quick solutions. Most stumbled through heavy and personal topics online, without the benefits of physical proximity, making them even tougher to navigate effectively.

During this process, racially marginalized leaders engaged with their workplaces and colleagues in new ways. The increased awareness and commitment to equity was an important, though delayed, shift at work.

However, it directly and indirectly required added emotional, mental, and physical labor for people of color. Companies looked to the experiences of their staff of color to inform that work. Hearing the voices of those most affected by the call to action was important; however, sharing those perspectives for the edification of organizations was and is work—hard work at that. While these team members carried the burden of witnessing the violence that was occurring, they also were expected to carry the weight of processing the professional version of bias for the benefit of those who had been woefully unaware.

When we consider the weight of this work as a baseline and add to that the effort required to be conscious of the ways in which we engage professionally, the task can become overwhelming. There has been a lot of pain and suffering that our communities have experienced, which is compounded for leaders who identify with those communities with every act of violence. It does not go away with time; it just layers on. It calls for an unmatched level of resilience that is accessible only by facing and moving through such persistent, recurring challenges.

WEIGHTED PERFORMANCE

Track stars often practice sprinting while harnessed to a parachute; the wind they create with their forward movement provides increased resistance in getting to the finish line. Others may wear physical weights around their ankles or arms to build muscular ability and to improve outcomes when they are not weighed down.

The resiliency of leaders of color is developed in a similar way. The weight of the world falls on our shoulders, and we carry that weight in our day to day. A particular type of resolve is required to work through to-do lists, deliver on projects, set and facilitate agendas, and supervise or collaborate with coworkers when societal realities strap a parachute on your back as you run. Given the vast disconnect that can exist between the violence occurring and Monday's staff meeting, we can start to question what it's all for.

Leaders of color still show up, perform, and persist in the workplace despite this heavier load. We run the race beside others unfettered by ankle weights or unobstructed by hurdles in their lane. And we keep up nonetheless. The challenge is that everyone thinks we are all running the same race, without realizing that some have additional obstacles blocking their way or extra weight to carry. The act of getting to the finish line is analyzed far more often than what it takes to get there. Even more difficult to uncover is how "what it takes" looks different for different people. How often have performance reviews explored how societal loads may affect one's ability to meet outcomes and expectations? Or which supports or processes could be established to better take that load into account? On the other side of this, when outcomes and expectations are achieved and surpassed, are performance review processes set up to notice and acknowledge the ankle weights one might be wearing as they achieve those successes?

There is power, talent, and skill in navigating one's career while carrying this heavier leadership load. BIPOC leaders navigate challenging work environments and flex through systemic barriers under these circumstances every day. Therein lies a deep commitment to leading with integrity and impact that uniquely emerges because of these difficult conditions. Though incredibly challenging and, unfortunately, personally detrimental at times, this reality highlights the determination and leadership strength that racially marginalized leaders can exhibit. Skillfully focusing on the task or job at hand in spite of the harmful realities surrounding and impacting us is an overlooked contribution to our organizations. Companies truly benefit from our ability to do this, though it is uncertain how sustainable that practice is for us individually.

UNWELCOME EMOTIONAL RESILIENCE

By tragic default, leaders of color maintain an emotional resilience that is critical to organizations navigating change and crisis. As we have explored, resilience is increasingly an important tenet of effective leadership. We live in tenuous, uncertain times that require fortitude to move toward a vision obscured by continuous tumult.

The fact that BIPOC leaders have had to develop this resilience is troubling. It exposes an unjust and dangerous world. However, we must also recognize the expanded leadership capacity these leaders acquire given these realities. These transferable abilities lend themselves to much more meaningful leadership challenges such as building work environments that illuminate all perspectives in fulfilling ways. This added load indirectly has prepared us to do the hard work that leaders are often called upon to do. No matter the complexity, level of conflict, or propensity for tension when undertaking a challenge, racially marginalized leaders have witnessed worse. There is little in professional environments that can truly catch these leaders off guard.

These untapped leaders can carry an admirable steadiness within them, a constancy of character cultivated merely by navigating a life that requires processing the consequences of racism and oppression. If we were knocked over by every unnecessarily violent end to a Black or brown life or side-swiped by moments of seemingly harmless yet racist exchanges in Central Park, we wouldn't have made it to where we are. Racially marginalized leaders have no choice but to get up and get back in the game, tragedy after tragedy. Through that process, we develop a resiliency that allows us to press through every work setback or challenge. How you recover from significant business challenges is a sign of your aptitude for leadership, and this mindset unfortunately has become second nature for people of color. The leadership birthed out of the ongoing personal toll that societal racism takes on us is personally devastating. It's a legacy that we don't want nor should it be forced upon us, yet it exists and should be named.

WHAT THIS MEANS FOR YOU

As you consider your leadership, note the load that you carry or have carried. What weights are you wearing around your ankles? In what ways are you running with a parachute on your back? This true leadership moment asks you to name and identify those weights, notice the impact they have on you, and communicate that impact in some way in the workplace. Don't let the load crush you over time, because if left unchecked and unexamined, it will.

How can you prioritize your well-being when your workplace may not notice the added load you carry? How can you meaningfully build relationships with coworkers, direct reports, or supervisors to offer your support during tragic moments? How can you contribute to a work culture that recognizes and leaves room for the realities of being human in a difficult world?

There is an opportunity here to exercise leadership by setting firm boundaries and asking for support when needed. Say when you are going to put down some of your weights so that others know what you have been carrying all along. This can feel challenging, particularly in workplaces that have not historically acknowledged the influence and impact of experiences outside of work. However, if you don't draw the line, it might not get drawn. If you don't say, "I need more time to deliver on this. I am still processing recent events," then the unspoken expectation is that you deliver regardless of how you process tragedies in the community.

You can also contribute to creating a culture of care, particularly if your leadership load is not as heavy as others. Determining how you can support colleagues during difficult moments rather than avoiding those tough moments can go a long way. Don't know how? Ask them what you can do. Or merely mention that you are available to offer whatever support is needed. Oftentimes, someone noticing the weights you carry can serve to alleviate their heaviness.

WHAT THIS MEANS FOR ORGANIZATIONS

As the onslaught of tragedy continues across communities and our society as a whole, organizations must prepare themselves to meaningfully support the people who spend the majority of their time within their proverbial walls. We are no longer living in a world where compartmentalization is possible. (Have we ever lived in a world when that was healthy?) It has become increasingly clear that people carry their experiences, struggles, hopes, and fears into work every day, regardless of their to-do lists and responsibilities. The load is heavy, and operating as if that reality does not exist is not sustainable.

To build healthy organizations, companies must invest time into and allow space for life and humanity to coexist. To truly create equitable workplaces and cultures, the inequitable leadership load must be acknowledged. This could be through building malleability and flexibility into goals and metrics to account for unexpected traumas. If there is a race-based mass shooting or any disturbing news update, cancel the team meeting. Push back the deadline. Work will still feel urgent, and some aspects might seem as if they cannot be rescheduled, but build a culture that tries. Urgency, in many cases, is manmade, so these moments are a worthwhile test of our interpretation of the term. Supporting team members during moments of undue stress will likely pay more dividends than plowing forward to preserve a predetermined timeline.

Hesitation about such flexibility undoubtedly may emerge, particularly given how often tragedy occurs and how varied it can be. A trust question may emerge—are employees taking advantage of such a culture and saying that they need flexibility and delayed deadlines even if they don't feel affected by external tragic events? Where is the line? At what point is it counterproductive and disruptive? These questions are understandable and also might expose some broader cultural challenges. I'd argue that if a work environment invests in the authentic well-being of its participants (beyond yoga Wednesdays), then its participants will invest in the work.

Acknowledging the real lives of diverse teams is essential for organizations to thrive to their full potential. Incorporating time and space for those lived realities to exist and breathe in the workplace can be transformational. Let staff know their load is seen. Move beyond company statements and back up those words with actions: create confidential support groups if your organization is large enough or implement genuine individual "check-ins" with staff to identify how to uniquely support them.

Of course, there are limitations to the support an organization can provide individuals, particularly when it comes to healing from societal trauma. It is not necessarily a company's role to take on that work. Offering health insurance for supportive services is a baseline, as is not contributing to the harm. Disregarding this heavy load as if it doesn't exist or engaging in performative communication without genuine effort to make the workplace more palpable to navigate in the aftermath of tragedy is also harmful.

Consider what policies and practices may aid or inhibit the support of staff whose leadership load may ebb and flow as life does. It can be assumed that all team members at all levels of an organization experience a heavier load at some point in their careers. Organizations that can operate less rigidly and more aligned with the realities of life will be better off with healthier and more committed teams.

PART III

LEADERSHIP LESSONS FROM AN ESSENTIAL STANDPOINT

10

LEADING WITHIN YOUR ZONE OF UNTAPPED CAPACITY

In part II, we had the opportunity to dive deep into the foundation of leadership and examine how it led to limited interpretations of leadership itself. We expanded our analysis to include voices that had been systematically excluded in the conversation, both explicitly in nineteenth- and twentieth-century leadership and more implicitly in present-day dialogue. We learned from untapped voices exercising leadership across sectors through a variety of methods, all offering unique insights for us to consider as we explore our own leadership journey and impact. We now explore how we can apply some of these lessons in real time, on individual and organizational levels. The result is a more connected, aware, and effective leadership approach that accounts for the complexities and realities in our world and, by default, in our offices.

Given the narrow lens through which we have examined leadership, the charge now is to purposefully seek what has been overlooked. What are you missing in your own leadership? What have you not considered? What has been informed by what you have been told, possibly by leaders with whom you don't identify, versus by what you have experienced or know to be true through other modes? These parts of ourselves and our leadership deserve visibility. They should be part of our toolkit as we address the complex challenges ahead and work with others who are seemingly different from us.

In Gay Hendricks's book *The Big Leap*, he discusses the quest to operate within one's "zone of genius," a place where you flow, thrive, are most fulfilled, and are likely to contribute work that is highly distinguished from others. According to Hendricks, many of us end up finding ourselves in our "zone of excellence." We become good at what we do. We excel. We can do the work and even receive accolades for results. But there is something that falls short. There is an aspect to the work that might leave us unfulfilled or may extract more energy than it gives. Nonetheless, we stick with it because we realize we're good at it.

What ultimately happens, however, is that we hold ourselves back from reaching our zone of genius—that place where the work comes easily, and we enjoy it to the point that it does not feel like work. It fuels us as we fuel it. This arena is where we have the opportunity for most impact. However, if we are to learn from the leadership of those marginalized in workplaces, we uncover that one's zone of genius actually exists within what I call one's zone of untapped capacity. There are aspects of ourselves, our perspectives, and our experiences that we don't consider when exploring our zone of genius because they have never been part of the narrative for leadership. Thus, we cannot adequately identify our zone of genius until we have explored the untapped capacity we hold.

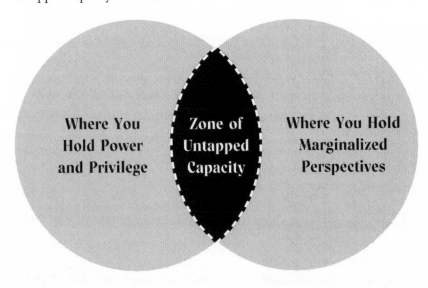

Where You Hold Power and Privilege — Zone of Untapped Capacity — Where You Hold Marginalized Perspectives

The zone of untapped capacity sits squarely at the intersection of where we experience the world with our power and privilege and where our marginalized identities offer a powerful standpoint from which to lead. The parts of ourselves that do not fit into traditional notions of leadership, which are overlooked in dominant work cultures or muted in challenging environments, provide us with a work and life experience that is more connected and real. These experiences yield assets and skills that should be utilized to inform the nature of leadership and are precisely what we need to contribute

UNTAPPED VOICES

At the end of the day, I perceive reality through the meaning I draw from what's happening to me. I do believe at the very least I can influence my own experience through my thinking, through my being. So if I'm advocating for a different paradigm of leadership, what does it really mean? Beyond the big words, what does it practically mean for me? And in order to answer that question, I have to dig deeper because I recognize how much I am biased. The way I was brought up, the way I experienced my career—I'm very biased by my past. It is my job to first identify and articulate it for myself and then for the world—what is it that I bring to the table that is uniquely mine? This makes me tune in to the price of not having diverse leadership to learn from, examples of people to relate to on a deeper level to redefine what's possible for a larger number of people, and the necessity of embodying leadership for others.

In our otherness lies our strength, superpower, and our secret ingredient, which can be expressed in many different ways. We just need to learn how to incorporate the fitting combination to achieve goals at hand and be open to multiple-choice solutions. I'm willing to bet that rather than trying to select people that tick familiar boxes, decoding and unleashing everyone's genius and masterfully channeling it toward common goals will yield better results for the proverbial corporate bottom line. Maybe that's a leadership skill to zoom into.

—Elena, executive in music licensing, Asian

at work. This is what has an impact, creates change, and builds organizations that are strong, inclusive, and long-lasting.

We should leverage all the resources we have when engaging in team meetings, pitching project ideas, and building workplace culture. Not utilizing our full perspective or downplaying aspects of ourselves ultimately does a disservice to our reality and our progress toward an impactful future. We are withholding insight that is essential.

To examine the zone of untapped capacity, look no further than this book, which is an output of me working within my zone. Like for many of us, 2020 was a core-shaking year for me. I had given birth to my second child four days before we entered into lockdown due to the COVID-19 pandemic. With a preschooler and a newborn at home, the pandemic was completely disorienting; the required global pause left a lot of room to stop, reflect, and reevaluate priorities. However, it wasn't until George Floyd's murder that I was jostled into realizing the subtle ways I had been complacent and complicit in the worst parts of our current reality. I have spent decades studying and facilitating leadership. I found success in developing leaders across all stages of their careers, from high school to the executive level. I have thrived in leading group learning environments, bringing cohorts of people with multiple perspectives and diverse backgrounds together for tough conversations about leadership.

That moment in 2020 exposed the ways I molded and muted myself to internalize and facilitate leadership frameworks that were not built by people like me, that did not even have people like me in mind when they were created. In reading all the canonical studies and creating curricula and leadership development programs based on frameworks designed by men who don't look like me, I realized that I had been stretching and contorting my authentic self to make the work fit and had never considered that reality because I was excelling at it.

Although it may seem like a stretch for me to consider my actions complicit in the violence we witnessed, I saw a connection. In my corner of the world, in my own sphere of influence, I had not been doing everything I could to bring my unique perspective and experience to the work. I had not considered my standpoint as a biracial Black woman and mother as pivotal. I worked with what was in front of me and exercised some of my natural talents in other ways but never in the way needed most—with my marginalized perspectives at the center. It was a critical moment to deeply evaluate how

I spend my time and talent in my career, to move away from complacency about what has been handed to me and inherited from the past and toward what the world sorely needs now.

I explored my own zone of untapped capacity by naming the ways in which I have power and privilege as defined by current standards—a doctoral degree in education, executive-level title, middle-class income, social capital through diverse connections—and the ways I hold marginalized perspectives—being biracial, being Black, being a woman, being a mother. I then considered the ways I could leverage my privilege to lead from my marginalized perspectives and exercise my expertise. Operating in the world of leadership, the exercise called into question all the concepts that emerged in this book. Purposefully centering these perspectives, which I originally set aside, to do the work allowed me to examine the entire industry from a vantage point that I have not seen many discuss.

Tapping into my untapped capacity uncovered my true zone of genius. It was a step beyond merely finding the work that moved easily through me. Discovering your flow and operating in this productive zone is one thing. It is quite another to direct those efforts toward the worthy and impactful cause of bringing your full self into your work. This discovery exposes purpose much more clearly, and that purpose is where we lead meaningfully toward the just and equitable world we hope to see.

Within this zone of untapped capacity, we unearth the deeper layers of leadership, the unsaid components that might offer us some answers to our persistent challenges. This revolution is our only chance to lead differently, to shift away from what is handed to us and toward what emerges within us. Our own genius often lies in those overlooked places. It exists in ways that the external world may not notice because it developed in the margins, unsolicited, and weighed down by societal marginalization. What results, then, may not represent or account for the full nuances of what we can offer.

ACCESSING YOUR ZONE OF UNTAPPED CAPACITY

This zone of untapped capacity looks different for all of us and deserves an audit to crystallize how we should lead when building the teams, organizations, and world we want to see.

Although we've explored the deep well of untapped capacities of BIPOC leaders in this book, this reality exists for many, including women, LGBTQ+ community members, people with visible or invisible disabilities, older workers, and others who have been placed at the margins of leadership as a result of the dominant narrative, which we've cultivated since the nineteenth century. I would even argue that there is a zone of untapped capacity for those without traditionally marginalized identities who have not been able to access the full complexity of themselves because of the inherited expectations of what leadership should be.

To explore where your zone of untapped capacity may exist, ask yourself the following questions.

- In what ways do I hold power and privilege? There are likely ways that emerge easily but dig a little deeper for things that you may not initially think of as privileges. These privileges are often disregarded because they are inherent and hard to discern (e.g., good health is an overlooked privilege).
- What parts of my identity and life experiences are marginalized? You might gravitate to the macro-level identities that can be marginalized like race, gender, sexual orientation, language proficiency, and so forth. Also consider the more micro-level instances of marginalization—the moments when you might self-edit or contort your authentic and preferred self or style.
- How can I leverage my power and privilege to spotlight my marginalized perspectives at work? And for what purpose?

We can have a profound impact on our work by leveraging our power and privilege in a way that calls attention to our insights that would be otherwise marginalized. To really examine and redefine leadership, we must look at it through the lens of these moments. Leadership should extend beyond being at the head of a table or the top of an organization. It should also mean expanding and reimagining how we do things to better reflect the realities of our world. That means taking a good, hard look at our power and owning all aspects of its current iteration, whether earned or unearned and whether comfortable or not. That also means bringing in overlooked and even unpopular perspectives because they hold and represent the value of the untapped margins.

Innovation exists in those margins. Solutions exist in those margins. As leaders, we have a responsibility to stretch when possible into those areas that are traditionally shadowed, even if we are the only ones doing so, because only then do shifts begin to take place. If we continue to fall in line with what does not align for us, then those binding limitations will persist, keeping us from reaching our untapped capacity or our true genius. And the world misses out too. Others who may be experiencing the same misalignment keep on keeping on, in isolation, thinking that this is how things are and will always be.

Undoubtedly, however, most of us understand that we cannot fully bring our marginalized perspectives into work without some caution. As we explore our zone of untapped capacity and identify ways to account for and bring in our whole selves to our professional spaces, we must also concurrently assess the level of trust and respect established in that space to approach it effectively. The nature of marginalized perspectives often places them at automatic odds with other perspectives, creating friction in the environment when they are introduced. In low-trust workplaces, that friction can result in harmful responses and reactions. In spaces with high trust, that friction is interpreted as beneficial because the group then has a more accurate understanding of reality and can make more informed decisions as a result.

If you are in a position in which you hold notable power and privilege without many marginalized elements, this is an invitation to explore that dynamic a bit more. How can you expand your own perspectives to include the perspectives of those with marginalized identities? How can you move beyond saying that you'll seek those perspectives and actually put it into practice?

We all fare better when our nuance and diversity are spotlighted in the workplace. We strengthen our leadership by uncovering the ways in which we may not be accessing all of our talents and expertise because we think that they are not essential or may not be welcome. If we omit those realities, then we touch the surface of the work. For change to happen, innovation to occur, and cultures to shift, this deep, layered work is required. It is not easy, but as many of us know, not much about leadership is easy.

To best equip ourselves to lead effectively and impactfully, we must search for this zone of untapped capacity, we must be honest about our own untapped capacity, and we must cultivate action within that zone for others.

UNTAPPED VOICES

After George Floyd's murder, I really felt very strongly and really led with my heart. Everything under my control in marketing we shut down for Blackout Tuesday. We literally shut down. I was very grateful to have leadership that was really supportive. The president of my division was super supportive of what I was trying to do. Through that, we ended up creating a DEI [diversity, equity, and inclusion] task force that closely examined how were we addressing diversity within our company. How were we helping make sure that, in our staffing and recruiting, we are presenting a diversity of candidates to our clients?

And even though I wanted to be in the nonprofit sector, I knew that I was right where I was supposed to be at that moment, because as the director of marketing, I could effect change from my seat at the leadership table.

Often we think changemakers are the people on the street knocking on the doors, passing out the flyers, and rallying everybody to come to the protest march. And don't get me wrong, that is so super important. You need that. But I realized the role that I had at that moment was important because I was behind the curtain. I was sitting where the decisions were made and had the opportunity to inform and influence those decisions.

—Carole, director of marketing for a staffing
and recruitment firm, Black

LEVERAGING UNTAPPED CAPACITY IN CAREERS

As part of the process of operating within your zone of untapped capacity, identifying its purpose is essential. What is the point? Why leverage these standpoints to inform your work and career? Operating in this zone can address purpose in a few ways. It can allow us to operate with much more alignment in our day-to-day. The less we have to shed or put on as we enter the workplace, the more fulfilling the experience can be. The Great

Resignation of recent years has been more of a Great Realignment for many, a moment of reflecting upon and identifying what has not worked for them at work. Those who resigned likely set aside specific elements of themselves to align with processes, practices, and cultures in the workplace and ultimately discovered that self-repudiation did not work for them.

I'd venture to say that we all want to do work that is fulfilling and feels purposeful. Being clear about where your zone of untapped capacity exists can establish those guideposts. The "how" and "what" of your career can shift and adjust, but your "why" can rest in this zone. That "why" can direct us to engage with our work environments more intentionally, nudging or even pushing them to be more inclusive merely by spotlighting your marginalized experiences.

Our work can become all-consuming and play a significant part in our lives, making it easy to closely identify with positions. But attaching and identifying ourselves too closely to our professional roles and titles at work is unhealthy. Sure, Gay Hendricks's zone of genius can aid in identifying the type of work you love and thrive in, regardless of title or industry, and expand the possibilities by clarifying what you naturally flow with. Deepening that work within the zone of untapped capacity, you have the opportunity to engage in that same flow with added layers of genuine authenticity. The zone extends beyond tasks at hand—it elevates our full selves as an essential part of the equation. It honors and promotes the inclusion of any aspect of ourselves, our identities, or our lived experiences into the task at hand. That practice makes what we contribute to the world wholly unique. It essentially guarantees that no one else is doing the work you're doing with the same approaches and considerations you take, because only you hold that capacity. Talk about genius.

Keenly understanding your zone of untapped capacity offers you a unique vantage point from which to guide your career. It can cue you to the spaces where you can help shift culture, create change, and influence positively toward full potential. It can also alert you to spaces where you cannot. Understanding more vividly the ways in which your perspective and potential are underutilized or overlooked can expose environments that may be limiting your distinct leadership. We can attempt to do only so much in some work cultures. If we receive increased resistance through feedback and performance evaluations or if there are negative repercussions when our perspectives challenge the status quo, then we know it is time to look toward places that will invite those perspectives. Perhaps the greatest workplace failure is the unrealized potential of team members. Don't sit in that space for too long. The world needs your leadership to thrive.

CULTIVATING UNTAPPED CAPACITY IN THE WORKPLACE

Getting the best out of its people benefits every organization, resulting in employee retention, better and more consistent outcomes, and a culture of human performance that is fulfilling, challenging, and sustainable. Yet organizations often struggle to cultivate each person's best, even more so when its staff carry diverse and often marginalized identities.

What holds organizations back? One issue seems to be an innate hesitancy and avoidance of conflict, even when that conflict is productive, allows for difficult truths to emerge, and encourages the creation of stronger teams through trust. As we have witnessed in recent years, our views of the world have become increasingly polarized. "Cancel culture" has emerged as a hot-button phrase with fervent proponents and opponents, deeply pitting sides over what some may interpret as mere opportunities for increased accountability. We find it difficult to agree not only about opinions but also facts. There are eggshells being walked on, arguments skirted, and perspectives withheld to avoid uncomfortable conversations.

As groups, we are out of practice of having productive and authentic difficult conversations, or we may have never equipped ourselves to engage in such dialogue. This is amplified in organizational environments when (1) work product, outcomes, and deadlines take precedence and (2) leadership and power are intertwined, influencing the ability to have conflict, particularly in the face of a lopsided distribution of power. We are expected to achieve outcomes and are evaluated on meeting those outcomes: across all levels of an organization, we are constantly and consequently oriented toward processes and exchanges that get us there as quickly and assuredly as possible. Bringing in conflicting opinions and approaches and welcoming challenges usually is not part of the preferred process, and that is understandable. Sometimes, things just need to get done, and a straight line from

A to *B* is our best chance. But is that the best way to work? The question begs asking.

Our current relationship to leadership, power, and authority also limits our willingness and ability to engage in conflict. We often find ourselves tiptoeing around those with positional authority. We institute strategies to "man(age) up," even with the most welcoming of managers, because it feels like anything else would jeopardize the deference that is expected in authoritative relationships. In some workplaces, giving challenging feedback or even questioning workplace authority figures can be deemed insubordination (the term *subordinate* is also quite telling of how we view those on lower rungs of hierarchical structures). These practices cultivate our traditional interpretation of leaders on pedestals, untouched and unchecked because of the assumption that they hold these positions because they know best.

We tend to create a narrative in which conflict is messy, and we don't like messes. I'd argue that conflict is clean—it clears things up, spotlights dirt, and, if managed effectively with trust and respect, it washes the mess out, thereby producing our best work. Rather than interpreting conflict as something dirty to avoid or minimize or as something that detracts from achieving outcomes, we need to view it as a necessary component of the process to reach those outcomes. Conflict is additive. It is a benefit. And we should increase our comfort with it to evoke the zone of untapped capacity for our diverse teams.

Organizations can cultivate environments that promote untapped capacity during the initial engagement with candidates in the interview process. How can you craft interview questions that go beyond items on a resume and delve into the singular perspectives that candidates bring to their work? What do the candidates uniquely know that they learned holistically beyond their professional roles? Asking these questions offers hiring managers a broader, more comprehensive understanding of a candidate and introduces the candidate to the organization's interest in incorporating an individual's whole self into work. It inherently communicates what is valued at the organization, and early communication of that value encourages those contributions when a new employee comes on board.

Organizations can continue to incorporate their teams' zones of untapped capacity. Meetings are often the primary interactions that move responsibilities and tasks forward, so they carry a lot of weight and influence in how an organization gets things done. They expose a company's true culture: the good and the bad emerge for all to witness, and the nature of those engagements informs everything that follows. Do your meeting agendas allow room for overlooked perspectives and approaches to emerge? Do your processes encourage everyone to fully contribute from their unique best selves? Are agenda items limited to those of the facilitator, or do others have the opportunity to add discussion points? Is there a dedicated time for dissent, and how is dissent valued?

Organizations can bake in conditions that promote the inclusion of untapped perspectives and therefore untapped capacities. Because we are diverse humans, this naturally invites conflict into our conversations, but doing so with a purposeful, consistent process that permeates these exchanges contributes to the team's ability to trust that engaging in this way is safe. Even though such a process may feel like a time investment that detracts from the groups' abilities to achieve outcomes, it eliminates (1) the time wasted by the unproductive conflict that emerges when difficult conversations are avoided and (2) toxic work environments fueled by dominant voices or perspectives.

Leadership means distributing power so that perspectives usually excluded from typical top-down leadership structures have the same if not greater weight than of those at the top. It is a disorienting concept because it flips leadership models on their head. But organizations as a whole will be better for it. When marginalized perspectives are centered, when untapped capacities are uncovered, the traditionally centered perspectives and processes are also strengthened. The whole system becomes fortified. Competition and scarcity are often the perception, but they are a lie. This new distribution of power and leadership results in a greater measure of authority, investment, and significance for everyone at the table.

How can organizations ease this redistribution of power among those with most positional authority? It has to be built into the values structures, meaning it must be evaluated as part of the expectations for leaders to innovatively and thoughtfully facilitate teams and processes that allow for these untapped capacities to emerge.

Steering an organization toward certain outcomes—meeting numbers, improving the bottom line, and even responding to crises—requires leadership to a certain extent. But it could also merely require individuals who are good at achieving outcomes, sometimes at any cost and by any means. If we want to expand our traditional definitions of leadership, we should look to those who understand their own zones of untapped capacity. As we leverage what they can offer, they would also allow space and grace for others to operate within their own zones. The results are healthy organizations, fulfilling careers, and deeper, more meaningful outcomes.

11

EXERCISING
CONTEXTUAL AGILITY

Effective leadership must move beyond trait, behavioral, or situational leadership models and toward a more nuanced, inclusive, and impactful model of contextual leadership. At any given moment in our work, a lot is going on. We are not merely facing the present moment—the past, the people with whom we work and their own personal histories, and the interconnectedness among those factors fuel the reality of any current situation. Yet we orient toward tackling to-dos and projects superficially rather than assessing their undercurrents, even when that deeper understanding helps us better navigate toward success. That process requires more time, more attunement, and more critical thinking. It may feel like it deters from progress, but in reality, it is essential for progress.

As we have learned from the experiences and expertise of marginalized leaders, leadership requires keeping one's finger on the pulse of all aspects that contribute to an environment, not just what we see in front of us. Operating in stealth mode, contorting to align with dominant structures, and carrying different amounts of weight in the workplace all contribute to the context of our workplace. If we are to make a difference, we shouldn't gloss over or ignore those realities and how they affect us.

Leaders must understand the impact of context in every workplace, including their own imprint on that context. Context is not constant. It is ever-changing and dependent on the players in a space and the nature of their interactions. It includes all they bring into the environment, and what their interactions evoke. It makes our organizations come to life: it is what makes them hum. In truth, it should be what fuels company culture. When we tap in to that hum, into what's actually going on in the context of a particular group of people coming together to reach toward a goal, we tap into something special that mutually benefits the organization and those involved.

Contextual considerations are the critical missing piece of our popular leadership frameworks. The research that speaks to leadership traits and behavior are devoid of the role that contextual factors like race, gender, and other marginalized identities play. They offer surface-level strategies for leadership that are not equally accessible to all due to the societal contexts within which we operate. Even situational leadership, which by its nomenclature suggests that it considers context, falls woefully short in building leaders to respond to the situation most accurately. Its benign interpretation

UNTAPPED VOICES

I had to take on more responsibility in a role where I had to challenge myself and what I believed leadership was. For a long time I would say, "People will do what I need them to do if I show them that I'm willing to get my hands dirty, too. If I can lead by example, people will get on board."

I had to just recognize that there's a lot more complication to it than that. I think leading by example is part of what can help you build trust in leadership positions, but there are all these other things that go along with it. It's recognizing the social dynamics that are taking place in that system and what the relationships are like, and building relationships in different ways that add on to the trust that you're trying to build.

How do I get people to listen to me when they think they should have had the job that I had? Or how do I get people to listen to me when, despite my role and my formal title, they see me as an outsider? I've learned all of the nuances of leadership that go along with having those conversations, building those relationships, doing the work, and doing it at multiple levels across an organization.

—Tanya, clinical assistant professor in higher education, Black of a situation leans on stylistic suggestions for adapting to situations rather than guidance for better understanding what's actually going on.

Leaders must understand how identity, history, and other contextual influences play a role in different environments. You cannot effectively lead unless you have a keen awareness of what is going on. Workplace compartmentalization is a farce. No one checks baggage at the door; it is impossible. And to think that impactful events in society and our lived experiences do not enter our minds or interactions during business hours is naive. They are woven all the way through us, shaping the way we think, the way we communicate, the way we connect with others, and the way we make decisions. True leadership monitors the pulse on how these factors influence the work and how they move diverse teams to engage with each other. To be unaware of these realities is to miss the potential of such groups completely.

A contextual leadership framework considers how the past connects to the present and how those connections influence our view of the future. In leadership, each moment involves an ever-changing, real-time interplay between ourselves and the system within which we're operating. Systems could be whole organizations, divisions, teams, or even partnerships through supervisory relationships. We are connected to and influenced by

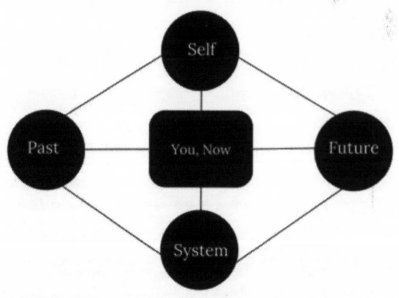

Contextual Leadership Framework

the system around us. We also influence the system in return. As a result, a certain dynamism occurs in that unique exchange.

By considering the past and future in connection to ourselves and these systems, we operate in the present more effectively. There's no prescription for leadership because there isn't one definition or one approach at any given moment. It involves understanding and appreciating all that occurs given the unique combination of factors. Leadership is not having all the answers in those moments but developing a deep awareness in those moments so you can respond and act more with more impact.

Contextual leadership involves strategies to (1) understand ourselves, (2) envision our future, (3) leverage our past, and (4) navigate our systems.

UNDERSTANDING OURSELVES

Impactful leadership requires deep self-awareness as a baseline. It is a must-have, not a nice-to-have. It is a prerequisite for leadership that is not emphasized enough. If we don't maintain cognizance of how we act and why we do so, then we run the risk of inhibiting our own impact and the potential of those around us. It should not be enough to produce results and achieve outcomes—leaders have a responsibility to take care in how they get there. In this twenty-first century, we cannot afford to approach work with the same priorities as in the 1900s. We must evolve and that evolution begins with understanding ourselves.

We typically understand that certain preferences and experiences make us who we are. Our preferred work styles, ways of processing, and communication methods differ, offering signs of that diversity. We also carry our lived experiences with us, some entrenched from our foundational years and earliest memories. These factors combine and thereby create our biases— toward what we know, what we agree with, and what we can understand easily. Building a critical awareness of the layers and nuances of our own selves becomes essential because otherwise we can affect people and organizations in ways we don't realize or intend.

Through detrimental processes such as code-switching and self-editing, marginalized leaders inadvertently developed a unique self-awareness as they audit their workplace communication and behaviors. To know what not to do, you have to know yourself to a certain extent. The opportunity here is for all to develop a deeper sense of self-awareness, to notice any differences between how we show up and how we are perceived. Building the capacity to understand how our decisions and behaviors may inhibit others is a tough task but a necessary component of any real discussion of leadership. Engaging in a reflective practice that uncovers the conscious and unconscious biases we all hold is a lifetime of work that we must accept when privileged with leading. It is not optional nor should organizations give a "pass" to top performers or those in positions of authority if they haven't done this work, as this plants the first seeds that produce toxic leadership.

What is critical to understand is that no singular antibias training or diversity, equity, and inclusion (DEI) retreat will accomplish this. Those efforts may kick off the work, but real leadership accountability happens internally in the day-to-day micro-moments. What have you done today to be less rigid in your way of doing things? What have you done today to understand someone else's approach or thought process? What have you done today that promoted someone else's unique leadership? What have you done today that has inhibited it? How do you know? (Hint: Ask.) We sometimes mistake "bias" as grand, sweeping, easily identifiable actions, but it lives in the minutiae. So we need to examine that minutiae and reflect on our role during such moments.

UNTAPPED VOICES

You have to know your audience. You have to learn your audience. You have to understand the room and the people that you're engaging with so that you can change your behavior. You can't expect anyone to change their behavior. You have to be able to do your best to speak their language and gauge if they prefer for you to be direct, if they prefer for you to be a little bit softer in your approach, or even if they need the first fifteen minutes of the conversation to be them venting after which they're ready to listen. You really have to take a moment to try to understand who you're engaging with so that you can change how you engage with them.

—Noelle, vice president in health care, Black

Understanding ourselves goes well beyond the Myers-Briggs Type Indicator or any other style assessment we might find out there. Those can be used as tools, barring any labeling or sorting based on results, offering some tangible takeaways for interacting with each other. Relying solely on those inventories, however, can deceive us into thinking that we have done the self-awareness work necessary to lead effectively. Although we might become more aware of style preferences, that surface information is only part of the puzzle. We need to keep digging.

Leadership is not easy, as many know, but it might be much harder than we think. We have to continually learn and unlearn, stretching beyond what we know into what we don't understand or agree with, and willingly engage in deep, critical work that exposes our true potential. We can likely get by—and even thrive and succeed—without doing this work. But the essence of leadership lies in that very moment—in the choice to stay engaged in the tough work even when current definitions of success don't necessarily demand it.

NAVIGATING THE SYSTEM

As we build upon our understanding of ourselves, we must then shift our examination to the environment around us. Assessing the nature of systems, whether that be teams, divisions, organizations, or even society as a whole, is critical to understanding how to move within those structures—or to move them entirely. Nothing occurs in isolation. Everything is interconnected. Being able to identify and evaluate those connections is a leadership practice stemming from marginalized leaders' hard-earned capacity to stealthily navigate toward their outcomes.

Building awareness of context, power dynamics, and culture in the workplace is essential to understanding how to leverage your own power and tap into the power of others.

There are different aspects of power at play at work.

- *Formal power*: those in positions of decision-making authority
- *Informal power*: those who exercise influence on decisions and culture even without formal authority

- *Societal power*: those who hold power due to societal hierarchies based on factors such as race, gender, sexual orientation, disability, religion, and socioeconomic status
- *Untapped power*: those who hold overlooked and underutilized power as a result of their marginalized perspectives

Contextual leadership invites leaders to engage in organizational power mapping. Marginalized leaders who operate in stealth mode are doing so because of a keen understanding of power and how to move with, through, and around it. Conducting a power map assessment is a helpful leadership tool to meaningfully move teams and organizations toward outcomes or to navigate systems confidently toward change.

You can usually examine formal power by looking at your company's organizational chart. Most commonly, those at the top of the chart have the most formal power. As you look at your organizational chart, make connections of ways you have observed informal power at play. Who has whose ear? Who seems to have a lot of say in meetings? Who has a lot of influence and with whom? Whose ideas get implemented? You may identify yourself in response to some of these questions or you may identify others.

A tricky but important step is to assess the societal power that can also influence your workplace. Our organizations are not divorced from larger societal contexts. Consider for yourself when and how issues of race, gender, ethnicity, sexual orientation, disability, religion, and other factors play out in power dynamics. The ways are often implicit, so it is important to clear assumptions as much as possible. Although the conversations might be difficult, leadership demands that we ask ourselves these tough questions or, better yet, that we have these discussions as a team.

Finally, take stock of any aspects of yourself that feel marginalized at work. It could be in connection to your identities, your work style, lived experiences, or anything else that gets set aside from nine to five.

Once you map the power in your organization—including your own—you can find ways to test the boundaries in an effort to make meaningful workplace shifts. Why not say the difficult observation that is on your mind in the next meeting or one-to-one with a supervisor? Why not contribute the thought that diverges from that of the group when the dominant line of thinking doesn't resonate for you? Why not connect with workplace allies to better understand your workplace power map assessment? If you have any formal or informal power, it is even more important to unlock your untapped power to effect change and make deliberate efforts to uncover the marginalized power of others.

To shift and expose the power that exists in the margins, we must integrate those margins into the core of our work. You may encounter headwinds going forward, so assessing the dynamics and interplay in the environment is essential for determining when and how to move. But these contributions alone are crucial enough to consider acting upon them.

LEVERAGING OUR PASTS

As discussed in previous chapters, we may find that our histories inhibit our understanding of our current reality, limiting what we think is possible for our future.

All of our interactions are informed by our pasts, whether we are aware of it consciously or not. We interpret the world and our strategies for thriving in it based on past experiences. It can be illuminating to explore how the foundational experiences you had as a child influence you at work. We expect the distance of time to weaken that influence, but those early moments of identity development stay with us through adulthood. We bring our often-invisible pasts into the workplace, as do all of our colleagues. Similar to the image of the iceberg often used in professional workshops, we experience only what is outwardly visible in behavior, yet underlying that behavior is decades of lived experience that scaffold into the present. We seldom learn such things about each other given the nature of our work-focused and outcomes-oriented roles. As a result, we don't investigate or even wonder about the backstory of how someone in front of us presents, thinks, or behaves. And they don't know our stories, either. At times our icebergs collide and, in those moments, we can experience an abrupt disorientation, wondering what transpired when others behave in ways we don't expect, given our above-water interpretation of them.

We typically think of the part of the iceberg that is visible without considering deeper commonalities or differences that exist below the surface. We rarely operate with the full picture and that limits our potential as teams and companies. We are ignorant of the full breadth and depth of what makes us who we are because we prioritize the here and now and the work at hand. It is a missed opportunity for impact because underneath the surface are the deep-seated values and motivations of team members. Their fuel and fears are tethered to something in the past; understanding those elements in another person is the key to understanding how to lead them or, better yet, how they can exercise their own version of leadership.

Beyond the histories of the individuals who make up a workplace is the history of the workplace itself. Understanding and exploring a company's past can provide insight into how to thrive there today. Organizations inherit many of their structures, processes, and policies. We typically don't question those practices because "that's the way it's always been done"—even if most in an organization are unlikely to know the "why" behind the "what." Examining a company's origin story—particularly large, long-standing companies—and the organization's trajectory—especially during pivotal societal moments—can offer clear insights into the values and motivations of the system as a whole. These systems become living ecosystems as those who came long before us establish elements that outlast their tenure.

If we are to lead companies or teams effectively, we also need to establish a deeper understanding of the system's past. An unknowing force that guides the present work, an organization or industry's history doesn't check past baggage at the door. Those systemic histories are set in the culture, the artifacts, and the track records that are established over time. To lead is to understand the nuance that an entity's history brings to the present. The history is not neutral—it has been crafted and fueled over time by people who mark it with whatever perspectives they bring into the work. Just as there are opportunities for us to unlearn some limiting interpretations of leadership, organizations likely have similar lessons to unlearn. If we have narrowed the way we lead, we have likely narrowed the way in which organizations can operate as well.

Becoming comfortable with critically facing that history to identify what elements no longer serve a company, its people, and its purpose is an essential leadership practice. It is even tougher to do when you have contributed to designing and executing elements that no longer serve a purpose. Some people develop personal attachments to the way things are, struggling to let go of outdated processes and policies that ultimately hold others and the organization back.

ENVISIONING THE FUTURE

We can't achieve inclusive and innovative workplaces by preserving the status quo of those environments. Understanding what is not working helps us define our aspirations and outline what is possible. As we examine our past to inform our present, we also build a bridge to our future. Imagining the future that we want to see and establishing the mechanisms and environments that will help us get there are essential to leading out our purpose. This process also builds organizations that can withstand uncertainty and mold and shift as necessary to achieve outcomes inclusively.

With a direct line from our past to our present, the future of ourselves and our organizations deserves thoughtful and hopeful consideration. That envisioned future requires a critical examination of what is and is not working in our current realities. It requires optimism, collective work, and imagination. We first have to imagine this for our own lives and careers, but we also need to create toward the future organizationally.

To understand what we'd like to see in our future work and leadership, we must examine and break through the limitations of our past. In what ways can we operate differently that we may not have seen or experienced in our careers thus far? Are there ways to reimagine leadership that are more resonant with who we are rather than what we have been told? If we don't creatively question current realities with a view toward building the types of organizations, missions, and work that are inclusive to our whole selves, then we continue to cultivate much of the same. Perspectives will continue to be marginalized and disparities within the top roles will continue.

It is hard to see what we haven't already seen and equally hard to unsee what we have already seen. Our interpretation of leadership—in connection to positions, roles, and individual people—is difficult to unlearn. If leadership isn't "this," then what is it? It's hard to pinpoint, so the debate about it continually abounds. As such, reimagining leadership and envisioning how we can redefine it in the future is challenging. It is a worthwhile challenge, nonetheless, and calls for our attention, examination, and discussion. In the process emerges the future.

As we consider how looking to the future informs our present leadership, the future asks how we define our ideal life and our ideal work. Surprisingly, we have the answers now. We know how we want to ideally live our lives and engage with our work. We know how to describe holistic work environments that support our success and help us thrive. We can name what workplace cultures should include to cultivate our leadership and the leadership of others. The challenge, however, is how to put those ideals into practice, and in that much tougher endeavor is the likelihood that unideal elements will remain. That is OK, for we can build around them. We will thrive despite them. Yet part of leadership is specifically naming those ideal elements that don't exist in our current realities and taking steps to bring them in. If we don't do something to create the leadership we want to see, no matter how small, then we perpetuate status quo approaches that may not benefit us.

We should connect our own micro-level visions for the future to the macro-level future that is possible, for what we want to see from our unique vantage points plays a role in bringing about larger-scale ideals. Only in this way will we shift and morph into a future that is fully equipped for impact.

To further effectiveness in leadership, you must also envision the future of the system—the team, organization, industry, society, whatever it may be. We have to move beyond the self and into the collective in a functional, thoughtful way. Leadership understands that we have the agency to create what we imagine in ways that extend beyond ourselves and that this is essential work. It is not about self-preservation or individual success. It is about building a future that strengthens the systems within which we operate and establishing the structures, frameworks, and processes that can outlast us and support those who follow. As leaders, we hold a responsibility to this work of leading our systems in ways that extend beyond our own benefit. If we are not doing so, then are we really leading?

BUILDING CONTEXTUAL AGILITY

The true art of leadership is exercising the agility required to understand the many factors contributing to a particular scenario and responding to them. Understanding histories, futures, systems, and ourselves is one step. The essential next step is to understand the ever-changing interplay and influences among them all. Effective leaders must understand the interconnections and employ flexibility and awareness to respond accordingly in those dynamic environments.

A deliberate examination of those connections may uncover untapped innovations and equitable practices that build stronger, more impactful organizations in the future. As we currently operate, we don't usually have the time or capacity to consider the full context as we move forward. We focus on the visible and immediate—the tasks at hand, the outcomes for the year, the bottom line. What is not visible or immediate are all the other factors that contribute to those things. The context is there whether we acknowledge and examine it or not. It is a factor in the equation, and leaders must do the math. This likely calls for a commitment of time, energy, and additional resources, but leadership requires us to hold the tension between cultivating the soil and picking its bounty. The produce doesn't bear if the soil is disregarded.

Marginalized leaders exhibit contextual agility almost every day at work, and this leadership ability is essential for teams and organizations. It is the exercise of accounting for the components described above and using that context to make decisions, adjust approaches, innovate for inclusivity, and cultivate many other benefits that we won't discover until we consider and leverage the interconnectedness of it all. It is a challenge, but that's as it should be if we are to confer the label of leadership to it. It calls on us to be able to approach our leadership with the humility of knowing we won't always have full context, but we can try to uncover it in the way we design our work.

UNTAPPED VOICES

Leadership really comes down to relationship building and getting to understand the folks around you and their individual visions. How does that bubble up into a potential collective vision? What are the pain points and pressure points and motivations that are relevant for each person in this kind of ecosystem that we're operating within? . . . It's much more of a cocreated—and should be a cocreated—process. Leadership to me ultimately is really facilitation. Leadership is about cocreation and creating a container for community. Can you create containers for that vision to be developed in to grow and blossom?
—Sara, self-employed in strategic operations
and culture design, South Asian

Contextual agility requires us to be in a constant state of learning. We are consistently assessing the environment. We examine the complexities of our relationships with others and the larger systems within which we operate. Weaving the connections between the self, the group, and the system is an essential leadership practice. Knowing that our pasts fuel our present and hopes for the future adds to our effectiveness.

DESCRIPTIVE LEADERSHIP VERSUS PRESCRIPTIVE LEADERSHIP

Effective leadership is oftentimes less about prescribing what to do and how to do it and more about accurately describing the complex realities of work and life. It is about keeping context at the forefront of all decision making, equipping reality to remain a player in the process. If you're not bringing in your full self or the full perspectives of others, then you're not leading. When leading in the present moment, strengthening the muscle to consider the past and future in your interactions with the system will have the deepest impact, no matter what decision is made.

Leadership frameworks and publications have long centered on prescriptive approaches to leadership: "Do this to be an effective leader. Don't do that to be an effective leader." There are of course some general dos and don'ts, but leadership may not be prescriptive. There is no one way to

UNTAPPED VOICES

Rather than jumping to judgment and/or knowing, I lean into curiosity. I have honed the skill of asking *good* questions that give me context to a situation. I have found this approach to show people as *full* beings who make choices that don't always serve them versus being just the total of their less-than-desirable decisions. Given this approach, I believe I have caught the attention of those in leadership who want to lean into the humanity of our work with the unhoused population.

—Shikira, chief equity officer for homeless services, Black

lead, nor one approach, hence the wide array of prescriptive approaches we see. With contextual leadership and agility, we are encouraged to describe more than prescribe—to focus less on what people should do and how they should do it and more on keenly observing real-time dynamics in context to better understand what you see and to elicit what others see. In that process, leaders fully engage others in their perspective and distribute the agency and ownership required for them to take action from there.

PACING TOWARD PURPOSE

Recalling the reflections from marginalized perspectives, we acknowledge that purpose has played and should continue to play a significant role in one's leadership journey. In addition to developing strategies for accurately assessing real-time context in any given situation, leaders must simultaneously understand the power of purpose as a navigational tool to move through that context. Identifying where we are and what we are working toward allows meaningful leadership to emerge, even (or perhaps especially) in times of chaos.

Purpose offers guidance, direction, fortitude, and motivation. Particularly during moments of challenge within limiting environments, purpose provides a polestar with which to orient oneself. One's purpose doesn't have to be a grand, existential objective or remain static over time. But as leaders, we have the opportunity to identify a goal larger than ourselves or our own individual success. It should not always be about merely getting the job done—we find more satisfaction in our work when purpose is involved. You have probably felt the energy of operating with purpose rather than on autopilot or for the sake of a job you don't particularly enjoy.

Getting clear on our purpose helps us make decisions meaningfully and effectively. It helps us to assess situations and move forward in a way that aligns with our values. As with marginalized leaders who work to pave the path behind them and to lend a hand to those following in their footsteps, working toward a broader purpose deepens our impact. Ideally, we all should work to make our organizations equitable and to make career attainment easier for others. You also may be motivated by a different purpose that is personally meaningful and fuels and guides your day-to-day actions.

Purpose must connect to something larger than mere individual career success. It extends beyond our roles, titles, and organizations. It encourages an activation of our whole selves as we consider what is truly important to us. What work do you want to take on that is not explicitly part of your job description? What is your purposeful approach to doing the work in your job description? What are the things you do that align with your values and who you are but that most others may not be aware of? Exploring these questions allows us to engage with others at work more meaningfully because more significant reasons inform the work than task completion.

Understanding how to navigate environmental limitations in the workplace is essential to pushing a compelling purpose forward. Work tends to prefer action, for high emphasis is placed on outcomes, tangible results, and performance, all of which must be achieved on a short timeline. To lead purposefully and in connection to others, thoughtful processes, intangible impact, and stillness must be valued equally. There must be pauses. We must have space for purpose to thrive and play out. Otherwise, we find ourselves on autopilot and missing out on deeper impact.

IDENTIFYING YOUR PURPOSE

We are well accustomed to mission statements, which name the reason we exist or do what we do. Companies use them as a grounding force and a polestar. You may have considered your personal mission statement or at least have identified why you do what you do. People might use purpose as stretch goals, guideposts, and sources of motivation. Defining purpose can sometimes be tricky, though. We are here on earth for a short amount of time, and we assume we need to figure out exactly why, so we sometimes look to our careers as a mechanism for purpose since we spend most of our time there. Although we might be able to name a grand, overarching life purpose for ourselves that also connects with our vocation, we might also find purpose in the small, everyday moments if we look closely.

Marginalized leaders often find purpose in supporting up-and-comers on their path, leaving opportunities more accessible than they found them. Mentoring, checking in, offering behind-the-scenes support, and thinking about ways to make their work and workplaces more inclusive are all purposes that run concurrent to broader career purpose for leaders of color. The fuel for this type of purpose is one of necessity. In challenging environments, marginalized leaders have learned to look out for each other and to operate under the radar to effect change. It is a purpose that all leaders should take on, especially for those positioned to do so not out of necessity but from a commitment to making work better for everyone.

Leaders should constantly ask themselves, "How can I leave this role and this company better than I found it?" How can you improve the workplace for everyone, especially for those who may experience it differently than you? What did you do today that benefited someone else at work? How can you establish a practice of identifying ways to support those around you? It is easy to get bogged down in the routine of work without considering these questions, but by remaining in this reality we promote the status quo, which can be challenging for everyone to navigate. If we are to talk about true leadership, then it must include a commitment—a purpose—that aims to improve conditions for marginalized leadership to flourish.

MOVING AT A PURPOSEFUL PACE

To lead effectively, leaders must mind the pace of their work and balance between action and inaction as a strategy for meaningful progress. If we're going to unlock potential and discover overlooked assets and expertise on our teams, we have to stop and look for them. When exercising the contextual agility required of effective leadership—building awareness of the connections between the past, the future, the system, and ourselves—we need to move among these contextual connections, often in real time. Our ability to do so is strengthened when we've had moments to pause and understand the full context of ourselves, others, and the organization as a whole. The term "agility" inherently implies moving quickly and easily; what is not noted is the preparation required to be agile. It doesn't happen effortlessly—it is a result of practice. There are moments of inaction—of pause—before agile action, the latter being dependent on the former.

Pausing can allow us to interrupt and examine practices perpetuating inequitable systems. That work is hard. It won't produce results quickly, and we have to build comfort with that. If we are clear on our purpose, then that comfort comes more readily. It also steels us when we face challenges and challengers. Moving at a purposeful pace, particularly when that purpose is long term, is a departure from what is traditionally expected of leaders. We are accustomed to visible results, and we want them fast. If you're pacing toward a meaningful purpose, though, you're likely not operating at the speed expected of you, and progress, if discernable, may be incremental. Friction emerges between the push to produce outcomes and resolve issues and the deep work of moving toward purpose. In that tension lies leadership. It requires us to play the long game in a short-term world.

Most things that are worth achieving usually are not easy to attain. Most things that are worth achieving are difficult to understand and challenging to tackle, so we default to what's easy. The shift proposed in this book—moving our interpretations of leadership away from traditional definitions—falls right smack in the middle of this idea. It is the opposite of a quick guide to leadership. It requires processing, questioning, and reimagining, all of which should not be rushed if these suggested shifts are to truly be integrated.

As of 2021, nearly 60 percent of leaders reported feeling used up at the end of the workday, a sign of burnout.[1] There are a host of factors that can contribute to burnout, but one undoubtedly is the propensity for overload—needing to do too many tasks and hold too many responsibilities at one time. We're bogged down, doing more with fewer resources. It's a setup that is not conducive to navigating at a purposeful pace. As such, leading purposefully and establishing the necessary boundaries to preserve a sustainable pace are essential, not only to work more intentionally but to stave off burnout.

PURPOSE OUTSIDE OF PROFESSION

We often connect and define our leadership within our professional structures. Given that we have inherited many of those structures, we may be capable of a lot more and inadvertently are missing out on all that potential.

If we explore purpose beyond professional walls, we can learn precious lessons that could inform and strengthen our professional purpose.

During a trip to Mexico, I participated in a temazcal ceremony, a traditional, pre-Hispanic healing practice originating with the indigenous Aztecs. It was a powerful experience of reflection and renewal grounded in connection to the earth, the sky, our ancestors, and ourselves. It challenged participants to stretch past physical and mental comfort to dig introspectively and uncover the messages you can hear only when all else is shut out. During the temazcal ceremony I almost immediately realized how disconnected we can become from lessons and practices taught by those who existed well before us. It feels like we depart further and further away from indigenous practices that have cultivated connection and survival. Interconnectedness holds so much more meaning than our computers ever could.

Our email inboxes overflow and our to-do lists become impossibly long—and for what purpose? Our opportunity to reconnect to this earth, to each other, and to our short time in this life is constricted by an overabundance of responsibilities that might not be entirely necessary. We won't find our purpose in our inbox. The temazcal ceremony made those aspects of life feel infinitesimally small when compared to the expansiveness of our time here, yet that smallness commands a lot of our attention. I came away with a renewed awareness of the powerful lessons that exist in places where we may pay less attention or may not even be aware. In those places important shifts happen to better align our work and life to our purpose.

CENTERING PURPOSE IN ORGANIZATIONS

When you think about centering purpose in organizations, you likely think of doing so with the organization's stated mission or vision. Teams should

---

TAP IN

What have been some unexpected sources for leadership lessons? What were those lessons? How can you incorporate them into your day-to-day?

---

rally around an organizational purpose, as it provides the direction and motivation for the work. However, individual purpose should enter the workplace just as much as an organization-wide purpose. To access our full dimension and make our lives at work more purposeful, particularly during the moments when we feel off-purpose, organizations must invite staff to reflect upon and incorporate their own personal purpose into the workplace. In that process, we present the aspects of ourselves that are typically left aside. These core parts of us initially may not have anything to do with the work at hand, but with their inclusion, we might find ways to incorporate that purpose more deliberately.

As we know, we spend a lot of our lifetime at work. Usually, when we experience a form of purpose at work, we tend to be more fulfilled with what we are doing. In that fulfillment comes motivation and drive to continue and, in some ways, it encourages a more mindful engagement with our jobs. Purpose disrupts autopilot as we connect what we're doing with something bigger and broader. It keeps us thinking about something larger than just ourselves and beyond our own individual career success, whatever it might be. Harnessing the motivation and engagement that comes with being personally connected to purpose is an asset to any organization interested in retaining a committed workforce. Supporting team members to engage with their purpose through their roles only strengthens their output and the organization's overall outcomes.

Considering our broader purpose and values and bringing them to work allows for a more aligned workforce. It encourages a more realistic engagement with work in which some of our most significant and most unique traits, gifts, values, and goals are folded into the process.

TAP IN

If you were to dissociate leadership from your professional workspaces and career, how would that change your definition of it?

13

LEADERSHIP LESSONS FOR ORGANIZATIONS

Many organizations have committed to examining how they can build more diverse, equitable, and inclusive workplaces where BIPOC leaders can feel a sense of belonging. To actually get there, though, organizations must be committed to assessing their leadership culture and examining whose leadership is explicitly and implicitly valued. We have to be ready to examine the foundation—the core—to understand the ways that we may be inhibiting or disregarding talent that is right in front of us. We settle for the ways things have "always been done" because we may not realize how limiting those ways have actually been. Our moment now—our true act of leadership—is to name the ways we must unlearn antiquated processes and practices and to actually take steps to do so. This is challenging work—it is slow, messy, and uncomfortable—and thus requires contextual agility and untapped capacity to be fully activated and engaged. In a holistic examination of leadership culture, organizations may discover how they overlook and undervalue the leadership contributions of marginalized team members. Until this comes under a microscope and is amplified on a megaphone, they will likely remain under the surface.

Marginalized leaders have navigated and thrived despite environments that limit their full capacity. They know how to move ahead even as flying conditions become more treacherous. They have supported organizations across the spectrum of inclusivity and have reached higher ranks in disproportionately small numbers. As a result, some assume that, barring those calls for diversity, equity, and inclusion (DEI) practices, we have done enough for change to emerge. Unfortunately, we have not. We have begun the ancillary work of diversity, equity, and inclusion, addressing the urgent aspects of the work with organizations and achieving mixed results. This work, however, must coincide with this critical leadership examination, which has often been divorced from DEI discussions. despite informing reality as its base.

There is urgency and importance in expanding our definitions of leadership in teams and organizations. We must cultivate opportunities to shift practices toward more impactful approaches that amplify critical standpoints that we otherwise haven't considered. We are facing complex, uncertain, and ever-changing challenges that seem to grow in scale each year. Why wouldn't we want to utilize all available human capital resources in response? That is not to say the response should be to overwork and overwhelm. The answer is quite the opposite—utilizing the full diversity of available perspective, approach, skill, and talent to fuel the work. In that process, efforts distribute and align with one's natural abilities. Basically, everyone should have room and encouragement to tackle their roles and leadership in ways that are most resonant and relevant to them. As a result, team members experience more personal and professional fulfillment, and organizations experience the exponential benefits that come from a thriving workforce.

We need a leadership reframe with marginalized leaders describing the picture and offering the strategies. There is expertise in the margins. There is innovation on the outside. There are new, effective ways of "doing things" gleaned from the sidelines.

We need everyone operating within their zone of untapped capacity, and we need people of color to lead the way. It's time. Without it, we'll continue to buckle under our most persistent societal challenges and miss out on creative and meaningful innovations, all as a result of our limited understanding of who can practice leadership and how it looks.

How can this be done? The following guidance supports organizations in establishing spaces that uncover untapped capacity and allow for full contributions from team members.

DIFFUSE POWER

Leadership, as we have come to interpret it, equals power. Centralized power siphons off leadership to only a certain few. As the data show, those few tend to represent only a small subset of our diverse society. Condensing power and leadership in this way may be one of the most identifiable mechanisms that limits the leadership of others in an environment. We, of course, need to examine broadscale ways to decouple leadership from power so that leadership can exist in a more expansive and evolving manner. But we can do something about diffusing power in organizations now, immediately impacting the way we work.

Heads of organizations, executive board members, and team leaders at all levels can diffuse their power in the following ways.

Describe the Work Rather Than Prescribe the Work

Oftentimes, top-rung leaders have a particular vantage point from which they view the moving pieces of an organization. Offering direction to team members is important to help them understand their role and their part of the organizational puzzle. Once direction is given, however, that is the opportunity to step from prescribing to describing. The "how" of team members' work processes should be up to them. The space to innovate, try new things, fail at new things, and work in ways that feel aligned and authentic is essential. This can, of course, create some points of friction, particularly when one's way of approaching work differs greatly from that of a manager. It also requires that all involved have a certain level of comfort with missteps and mistakes. But in these moments, a leader's job is not to step in, assert more control, direct team members to change the way they work, or take punitive steps to course correct. Leaders should describe what they observe, offer team members supportive feedback to cultivate their growth, and share suggestions for team members to consider as they decide their next move.

Leaders can lean on their expertise, organizational positionality, and contextual awareness to guide staff in their roles. This means moving away from providing all the answers or using their position and authority to dictate how something gets done. Command and control leadership is out, but some of its remnants persist when we hold onto power by controlling how our team members get to outcomes. Micromanaging still runs rampant and is a surefire way to stifle innovation and marginalize difference.

A logical next question is, What do we do when there are legitimate performance challenges? As staff onboard to their roles and are directed to the goals and outcomes expected for their positions within that larger puzzle, they should retain clarity about what they are expected to deliver. In those guiding conversations, providing direction toward clear outcomes and an early understanding of what kind of support is needed to achieve them is essential. If working agreements are clearly identified from the very beginning, then they are easier to revisit when the work strays off the mark. Interventions become less of a punitive tactic and more of an upholding of cocreated agreements established at the start of employment. Ultimately, performance challenges are easier to address when all parties begin on the same page.

Leadership is less about the supervision of others and more about a partnership with others. Positions on organizational charts should primarily describe the roles on a team. The connections among those toward the top should show who they are responsible for building a productive partnership with rather than who they are in charge of. When connected to the rest of the organization, we see whose expertise they lean on to get things done. Everyone plays their part and can exercise their expertise in the ways they prefer, and those toward the top of organizations are charged with facilitating the execution.

Of course, with shared power comes shared accountability. We must move away from all blame and responsibility falling solely on individuals at the top of organizations because that indirectly supports the idea of power sitting solely with those same people. Shared power requires shared ownership, and that ownership expects those who hold that responsibility to follow through on their part. Their part is critical for the team's success and the team will be looking for each member to take it on. Shifting that responsibility can be uncomfortable. We are accustomed to those at the top of organizations taking the heat when things get tough. We find comfort in believing it's *their* problem, and truthfully, that's what they're paid for. But if we want to make significant shifts in contributing fully to our work and making changes that reflect our authentic selves, then we must be ready for the shifted accountability that comes with shifted power.

Share the Context

We often hear about "top-down" decision making. Some organizations try to steer away from it, but at times, the larger a company becomes, the more you'll find decisions coming from the top. When the C-suite or the board meets about company-wide direction and decisions and strategies are discussed, some essential context occurs behind closed doors, a powerful siphoning off of knowledge. Important lessons around strategy, power, money, operations, and alliances are shared, and only a select few can engage in them. For anyone new to those spaces, it is the ultimate training ground for influence within an organization.

Those outside the room have no understanding of the stakes or how and why they inform those decisions and strategies. So it is a radical idea to expose some of those top-level conversations and decisions with the rest of a team. It goes against what organizations have ever done and even against corporate common sense as traditionally interpreted. It feels risky for some reason—those working for an organization may not be able to handle the full context of their company's reality, or if they are not on board with the company's new direction, their response and opinions might complicate things. These concerns reflect a likely reality, and in certain contexts they are enough to justify keeping certain conversations executive level or above. But at the very least, sharing added context for some decisions across all levels of organizations would benefit everyone as the work plays out.

Contextual leadership and agility ask us to integrate multiple realities and considerations into our work. Part of that practice is being clear and open about what contexts are being incorporated as we make decisions. Specifying them for our team and for those within our management structures (1) helps us to test that context and bolster effective decision making by inviting additional perspectives to give us the full picture, and (2) demystifies leadership in a way that cultivates the leadership of others. As teams better understand the factors that go into complex decision making and have some level of involvement in the process, they acquire knowledge and skills that are otherwise exclusive to those in the boardroom. They are exposed to workplace intellectual capital that, if embedded into processes and practices, diminishes that troubling trend of career success relying on "who you know" within a company.

Make Feedback Frequent and Multidirectional

Working with leaders from across sectors and at all levels throughout my career has revealed to me that most organizations find giving feedback a challenge. Somehow, we don't have the tools and mechanisms to engage in effective feedback or to build cultures of feedback. It is relegated to one-directional, once-a-year performance reviews with supervisors, if a company chooses to make use of them. As a result, we miss out on a great depth of capacity, a deficit that only deepens when there is no space or safety to send up feedback to those in positions of authority.

Feedback is essential in healthy organizations. Even more so when we work to diffuse power and fully engage the full capacities of our teams. If we are doing that well, then we are uncovering a rich diversity of lived experience, working styles, and guiding values. Those differences unleash moments when divergence can feel challenging, but there's an opportunity to strengthen as a result of that divergence if we take it. Such moments live in feedback—in exchanges that directly name what's working and not working given our unique perspectives and that find a way forward, leaning on a backbone of trust, respect, and areas of alignment.

If we are to uncover the untapped leadership of others, we need to embed feedback culture in everyday activities. Make feedback a tenet of the discussion of all aspects of the organization. Include it as a daily occurrence for team members to practice and engage with, and eventually it becomes second nature. Distributing the practice of feedback throughout daily exchanges shifts power from being one directional and confined to a performance review and expands into an opportunity in which we all can have the privilege of hearing and being heard as we build workplaces that are fully representative of all perspectives.

To use multidirectional feedback to diffuse power, you can take some of the following unconventional steps.

- If you are a hiring manager or recruiter, ask interviewees how they would suggest adjusting the interview process to best showcase their candidacy. Power dynamics are often most unbalanced in these pre-hire conversations. Imagine what could shift if candidates had an opportunity to share their feedback.
- When setting a meeting agenda, send it in advance to attendees with a request for feedback and edits. Agenda-setters hold a lot of power because they decide what is to be discussed. It is usually helpful for

one person to set the purpose and outcomes of a meeting, but the group should get to review and suggest changes.

- Embed feedback processes within those meetings. If you think about it, meetings are the pulse of an organization. They are the moments when groups come together to move toward a common purpose (ideally). These are prime exchanges and often the moments when certain perspectives are overlooked. Meetings should be facilitated and designed to get everyone involved and contributing. Explicitly ask team members what they do not think is working. Invite dissent and leave room to explore and unpack. Prepare for follow-up when complexity arises. Be cognizant of different processing times. If you have built a strong container, those who prefer more time to process will say so, and it is your role to facilitate that. Strong teams grounded in trust can engage in these discussions openly in the moment, but it may be realistic to set up parameters for individual feedback afterward. Invite team members who may not have contributed verbally during a meeting to share their thoughts privately.
- Overhaul performance review processes so that they include team members offering performance reviews to their managers. One-way performance reviews reinforce a traditional interpretation of leadership in which the person higher in the organizational hierarchy knows better than the person lower. Supervisors are the experts whereas direct reports are novices, and supervisors themselves are accountable only to those above them in the organizational chart. Power could drastically shift if performance reviews became a two-way exchange. When done well, performance reviews from a manager can transform a team member's growth, so their benefit is clear. In the same vein, however, a team member giving a performance review to a manager could create the same effect. Such feedback is not customary, yet leaders need it to be effective. Institutionalizing this exchange is essential. Given that some type of power dynamic will still exist, having managers share their own growth areas with their team members levels the power dynamic and hopefully encourages direct and open conversations.

Model True Authenticity and Vulnerability

The call for authenticity and vulnerability seems to have a particular limit. Some dominant practices and cultures still serve as an undercurrent for how we show up in the workplace. The stretch to align or conform can be deeper for those who are marginalized and underrepresented. But when we all show our cards, there is a subtle shift in power. We don't hold anything to the chest and come as we are. Work environments not only need to be receptive to that, but they must be conducive for it to happen. They must encourage all to play with their full deck exposed. Otherwise, those who can align with dominant culture most easily will have the upper hand.

This is a call for leaders to model true authenticity and vulnerability and develop the capacity to metabolize the authenticity and vulnerability of others. What does this look like? It looks like those with positional authority boldly admitting when they don't know something or when they are nervous, afraid, or hesitant about the decisions they have to make. It looks like shedding the armor and the artifice to expose the internal realities of leadership. It looks like an environment that invests time and resources into trust building, which may not directly connect to tangible outcomes on paper but will impact and fuel the work tenfold. It looks like teams leaning on those pillars of trust when colleagues bring their marginalized standpoint into the room by vulnerably addressing a microaggression or an inequitable practice. It looks like messy and difficult conversations that are not linear but are committed to exploring the contexts that affect the present moment.

Leadership requires us to facilitate these moments, to move toward authentic and vulnerable exchanges, and to tackle them head-on. It is easy to shy away from challenging conversations, stay on the surface of the work at hand, and gloss over realities for the sake of numbers and outcomes. But as we have explored, this practice has detrimental long-term effects, and it mutes the extent of the contribution that diverse teams potentially could make. If you are in a position of authority, show your hand by being honest and open rather than bluffing through the professional version of yourself.

INVITE, VALUE, AND COMPENSATE MARGINALIZED EXPERTISE

A primary goal of this book is to shift the spotlight toward the overlooked contributions and leadership strategies of those traditionally marginalized in workplaces. By nature of their positionality, these leaders carry a unique expertise in understanding and navigating the complexities of workplace realities. They often hold a keen awareness of interpersonal connections, power, strategy, and vision as a result of sometimes exercising their leadership behind the scenes or in micro-moments.

Organizations must take steps to widen their lens, explicitly inviting marginalized perspectives to the table. This initial step of inclusion must take place before we can move on to more meaningful action. Because most organizations have not been built with these perspectives in mind, they are often unaware of these overlooked capacities. We can seize the moment here and do the tough work of understanding the historical components that informed how organizations were and are still being designed and identify which aspects continue to have exclusionary roots even as they evolve.

As we have explored, there are exclusions and elements that are inhibited in all systems. For a system to take shape, some aspects are needed within it, and some remain outside of it. That is the only way to create a sense of order and structure toward whatever goal the system is designed to achieve. Although we may not be able to eliminate that reality, we can and must understand exactly what those systems leave out and for what purpose. We may find that we bypass some essential considerations primarily because we never noticed or considered them. We must admit that the system has been inherited, so we may be perpetuating exclusion, perhaps subtly, in how we interpret what belongs within the structure and what does not.

I invite organizations to examine how your policies, processes, and practices inhibit marginalized perspectives so you can better identify how to remedy this and create more inclusive environments. How does your organization inhibit perspectives in the following places or practices?

- Recruitment materials
- Job descriptions
- Hiring processes

- Onboarding processes
- Your organizational chart
- Your offboarding processes

There is both an opportunity and an urgency to analyze well-entrenched practices to uncover ways in which we perpetuate the marginalization of experiences.

As those instances are uncovered, not only inviting but actually valuing overlooked perspectives will be essential. Valuing such perspectives shifts power because there is a demonstrated understanding and acceptance that these standpoints are critical to an organization's success. These perspectives carry weight and importance. They require our attention and our curiosity. They should become just as important as traditionally prioritized perspectives, if not more. They should fuel the creation of agendas involved in setting meeting outcomes. They warrant the time and energy that important components of the work deserve. This is how diversity, equity, and inclusion actually play out—by distributing power from dominant approaches toward the equal but different power that exists in the margins.

To call for an emphasis on marginalized expertise without stating that this expertise should be compensated would be negligent. One core marker of value is compensation, not to be confused with *worth*, as our worth is not connected to our compensation. If we are to truly distribute power and reframe what we consider leadership to be—widening our focus to learn from and utilize strategies built from marginalized perspectives—then we need to distribute the compensation.

If employees are compensated for the expertise they bring to a position and their ability to do a job, this compensation also should extend to marginalized expertise when it contributes to an organization's success. It

---

TAP IN

What would it look, sound, and feel like if marginalized identities were to carry more weight in the workplace? What would change? What would remain the same? How would your processes, projects, and communication adjust, if at all?

---

has, unfortunately, become all too common for Black, brown, and many historically marginalized groups to be asked to guide organizations in DEI work without being compensated for that labor. An onslaught of task forces and committees have emerged in recent decades, and many companies benefited from the efforts of leaders of color in those moments. If we lean on these perspectives to strengthen our organizations, they must be compensated accordingly, and their roles and contributions should be equated to leadership.

AUDIT ORGANIZATIONAL LEADERSHIP CULTURE

Organizational culture is a big part of a business. There are officers committed to building culture within organizations, and they create retreats, mottos, traditions, visuals, and gatherings for this reason. Company culture informs productivity and job satisfaction. The better the culture, the more likely teams are to perform and the more easily employees can be retained. Given its importance, a lot is invested into cultivating and maintaining this culture.

A subdivision of organizational culture is leadership culture. Organizational leadership culture is not something overt or invested in—it just happens, and usually no one notices. As you read this, you might realize that you have never considered it. Leadership culture emerges as organizations decide who can take on top positions, move up in the organization, and take on more visible and consequential responsibilities. It is an undercurrent that speaks to how leadership is defined, whether loosely and diversely or traditionally and rigidly. Its pulse determines which leadership values inform decisions. We can learn a lot about explicit and implicit preferences when we audit this culture.

Auditing leadership culture offers organizations a deeper understanding of trends and biases that may occur when leaders are chosen. Some questions to ask yourself as you audit the leadership culture of your organization are:

- Who is considered to be "the leadership" of your organization? Are those individuals clustered at the top? Is your definition tied to titles or to management roles?

- Are there commonalities in leadership style, communication style, or work style of team members who get promoted internally? What types of behaviors aside from work product are preferred when considering people for increased opportunity?
- Are there informal connections that influence promotions or visible projects? Is there an element of "who you know" informing leadership decision making?
- How closely do those you have identified as leaders align with long-standing definitions of leadership?

Much of our organizations' leadership cultures exists implicitly. This explains why organizations are persistently fraught with disparate representation in executive positions. Only a subset of our society is being tapped for these roles due to how closely those individuals align with the traditional definitions of leadership. Auditing the ways that we may be perpetuating these disparities is difficult but critical.

MIND THE PACE, MIND THE SPACE

All of the ideas and guidance offered here and in previous chapters have two requirements in common—time and a supportive environment. This is a long game and we need it to have room to breathe. Harnessing the power of underrepresented and marginalized perspectives is a matter of nuance and complexity. Lived experiences are not uniform, even if there is commonality in their marginalization. When we make the important effort to bring those nuanced and sidelined perspectives to the forefront, they may test and challenge the foundations of our systems in ways that cause friction.

Organizations, then, must mind their pace when engaging with this process. It is urgent, but there is no rush. Speed only detracts and undercuts the deep work required to shift entrenched leadership definitions and practices. This very concept of taking our time will evoke resistance. As a broader culture, we don't like to move slowly; we value getting things done and getting them done quickly. We build efficiencies to reach desired outcomes as fast as possible with minimal effort or difficulty. The speed at which we communicate and the rate at which we achieve manmade outcomes

UNTAPPED VOICES

It all starts out with time. I have to have the time to be able to nurture and to be able to teach. Depending on what level you're at as leader, you have your regular day-to-day—you have the things that are in your job description—but it doesn't take into consideration the amount of time that it may take to develop someone. With that time that you spend with the individual, they see that you are invested in them. You are able to empower someone. Individuals might see themselves as being able to do a certain amount, but through dialogue, positive reinforcement, and showing them more, I can convince them that they can do much more.

Lack of time is an inhibitor.

At the end of the day, you have to make the time, and it has to start top-down. If we are not able to develop staff at all levels, then it's for naught, and it's not going to happen. It's going to fall apart. There's going to be a whole bunch of micromanaging going on. You're going to have to hire more people to try to micromanage, and your expenses are going to go up. It just doesn't make any logical sense for a business to be successful if you're not able to develop and empower your people.

—Noelle, vice president in health care, Black

through artificial urgency can be overwhelming. That pace prohibits us from expanding our understanding of how context impacts our work; it won't adequately invite the dialogue this work calls for. There's power in the pause. It can take the form of retreats, structured project debriefs and reflections, feedback exchanges, or other ways that deliberately halt the constant movement toward outcomes and encourage a breather of sorts to uncover the overlooked. That is the only way to make progress.

Establishing a work pace that allows for this leadership work gives rise to the importance of establishing an environment conducive to this process. No amount of allotted time fosters engagement if people do not feel safe doing so openly. The willingness to recognize how much trust exists on a

UNTAPPED VOICES

I think we are living through a paradigm shift in terms of what leadership looks like, and people who ascribe to more traditional leadership styles are uncomfortable. And that creates friction. I think the lesson is: become aware of your leadership story, and lead from there as you approach this struggle for meaning around leadership.

I would tell my younger self: "You do not need to adapt to other people's expectations in order to find a space to be heard. You should speak first, and the right space for you will materialize."

I would ask those who use traditional definitions of leadership (they could be BIPOC or non-BIPOC) to critically examine and possibly redefine their views and experiment with other models. See what happens when you allow others to lead.

Revise your definitions of quality, expertise, efficiency, and productivity. Ask for help from experienced professionals to guide you in these reflections; don't think that people in your organization who hold marginalized identities will know how to facilitate this work!

—Victoria, consultant for higher education, Latinx

team also indicates how ready groups are to widen their leadership lens and include perspectives that are usually excluded from professional exchanges. Creating opportunities for discourse are a moot effort if toxicity is not eradicated and trusted relationships have not been built. Of course, creating this container requires time and investment, which is ultimately why organizations should mind their pace and space to cultivate lasting change.

This is the moment to rethink leadership. We all should consider aspects of traditional leadership frameworks that do not resonate for us and consider exploring new models. This work is just beginning. There is much more to dig into during these next couple centuries in order to shift beyond the last couple. Just as theories from the 1840s permeate today's leadership models, what we change and revise now can reverberate for decades to come.

Let's lead differently.

NOTES

INTRODUCTION

1. Chimamanda Ngozi Adichie, "The Danger of the Single Story," TED talk, July 2009, Oxford, England, www.ted.com/talks/chimamanda_ngozi_adichie_the_danger _of_a_single_story.

2. Richie Zweigenhaft, "Fortune 500 CEOs, 2000–2020: Still Male, Still White," The Society Pages, October 28, 2020, https://thesocietypages.org/specials/fortune -500-ceos-2000-2020-still-male-still-white/.

1 THE SHAKY FOUNDATION OF LEADERSHIP

1. Thomas Carlyle, "The Hero as Divinity," in *Heroes and Hero-Worship* (1840).

2. Ibram X. Kendi, "The Heartbeat of Racism Is Denial," *New York Times,* January 13, 2018.

3. Francis Galton, *Hereditary Genius: An Inquiry into Its Laws and Consequences* (1869).

4. Meng Li, "What Have We Learned from the 100-Year History of Leadership Research? (Part II)" Lead Read Today, June 8, 2018, https://fisher.osu.edu/blogs/ leadreadtoday/blog/what-have-we-learned-from-the-100-year-history-of-leadership -research-part-ii.

5. Thomas Albright, Judson L. Jeffries, and N. Michael Goecke, "A Ruckus on High Street: The Birth of Black Studies at the Ohio State University," *Journal of Race and Policy* 9 (2013).

6. F. E. Fiedler, *A Theory of Leadership Effectiveness* (New York: McGraw-Hill, 1967).

7. James Dulebohn, William Bommer, Robert Liden, Robyn Brouer, and Gerald R. Ferris, "A Meta-Analysis of Antecedents and Consequences of Leader-Member Exchange: Integrating the Past with an Eye toward the Future," *Journal of Management* 36, no. 6 (2012): 1715–59.

8. T. A. Widiger, "Neuroticism," in *Handbook of Individual Differences in Social Behavior*, ed. M. R. Leary and R. H. Hoyle (New York: Guilford, 2009), 129–46.

9. Stephen J. Zaccaro, "Trait-Based Perspectives of Leadership," *American Psychologist* 62, no. 1 (2007): 6.

10. Merve Emre, "The Cosmic Laboratory of Baby Training," in *The Personality Brokers: The Strange History of Myers-Briggs and the Birth of Personality Testing* (New York: Doubleday, 2018).

2   LEADERSHIP IN ITS CURRENT STATE

1. Patrick M. Kline, Evan K. Rose, Christopher R. Walters, "Systemic Discrimination among Large U.S. Employers," National Bureau of Economic Research, July 2021, www.nber.org/papers/w29053.

2. Bryan Hancock, Monne Williams, James Manyika, Lareina Yee, and Jackie Wong, "Race in the Workplace: The Black Experience in the U.S. Private Sector," McKinsey and Company, February 21, 2021, www.mckinsey.com/featured-insights/diversity -and-inclusion/Race-in-the-workplace-The-Black-experience-in-the-US-private-sector.

3. Tiffany Burns, Jess Huang, Alexis Krivkovich, Ishanaa Rambachan, Tijana Trkulja, and Lareina Yee, "Women in the Workplace 2021," McKinsey and Company, September 27, 2021, www.mckinsey.com/featured-insights/diversity-and-inclusion/ women-in-the-workplace.

4. Daniel Kurt, "Corporate Leadership by Race," Investopedia, February 28, 2022, www.investopedia.com/corporate-leadership-by-race-5114494.

5. U.S. Bureau of Labor Statistics, "Household Data Annual Averages," 2021, www .bls.gov/cps/cpsaat11.pdf.

6. "2021 S&P 500 Board Diversity Snapshot," Spencer Stuart Snapshot, www .spencerstuart.com/-/media/2021/july/boarddiversity2021/2021_sp500_board _diversity.pdf.

7. Dev A. Patel, "In HLS Classes, Women Fall Behind," The Harvard Crimson, May 8, 2013, www.thecrimson.com/article/2013/5/8/law-school-gender-classroom/?page=2.

8. Leslie Shore, "Gal Interrupted: Why Men Interrupt Women and How to Avert This in the Workplace," *Forbes*, January 3, 2017.

9. "This Is What It Means to Lead," The Leadership Challenge, www.leadership challenge.com/Research/Five-Practices.aspx.

10. Barry Z. Posner, "Bringing the Rigor of Research to the Art of Leadership," The Leadership Challenge, www.leadershipchallenge.com/LeadershipChallenge/media/ SiteFiles/research/TLC-Research-to-the-Art-of-Leadership.pdf.

3 THE LIMITATIONS OF LEADERSHIP TODAY

1. Jess Huang, Alexis Krivkovich, Ishanaa Rambachan, and Lareina Yee, "For Mothers in the Workplace, a Year (and Counting) Like No Other," McKinsey and Company, May 5, 2021, www.mckinsey.com/featured-insights/diversity-and-inclusion/ for-mothers-in-the-workplace-a-year-and-counting-like-no-other.

4 A NECESSARY SHIFT IN LEADERSHIP AUTHORITY

1. "Feminist Theories of Agency," Brittanica, www.britannica.com/topic/ philosophical-feminism/Feminist-theories-of-agency#ref1049956.
2. "The State of Diversity in Nonprofit and Foundation Leadership," BattaliaWinston, 2018, www.battaliawinston.com/wp-content/uploads/2017/05/nonprofit_white _paper.pdf.

5 STEALTH MODE

1. Tim Reynolds, "Half of NBA's Franchises Now Have Black Coaches," Associated Press, June 1, 2022, www.nba.com/news/half-of-nba-teams-now-lead-by-black-coaches.
2. Santul Nerkar, "The NBA Has Lost Ground on Hiring—and Retaining—Black Coaches," FiveThirtyEight, June 23, 2020, https://fivethirtyeight.com/features/ the-nba-has-lost-ground-on-hiring-and-retaining-black-coaches/.
3. Vincent Goodwill, "How Black Coaches Are Still Struggling to Find Their Place in the NBA," Yahoo! Sports, February 27, 2020, https://sports.yahoo.com/how-african -american-coaches-are-still-struggling-to-find-their-place-in-the-nba-173318612.html.

6 CONTORTION

1. "The CROWN Research Study," 2019, https://static1.squarespace.com/static/ 5edc69fd622c36173f56651f/t/5edeaa2fe5ddef345e087361/1591650865168/Dove _research_brochure2020_FINAL3.pdf.

2. Courtney L. McCluney, Kathrina Robotham, Serenity Lee, Richard Smith, and Myles Durkee, "The Costs of Code-Switching," *Harvard Business Review*, November 15, 2019, https://hbr.org/2019/11/the-costs-of-codeswitching.

3. Salwa Rahim-Dillard, "How Inclusive Is Your Leadership?" *Harvard Business Review*, April 19, 2021, https://hbr.org/2021/04/how-inclusive-is-your-leadership.

7 THE DECEIVING NARRATIVE OF IMPOSTER SYNDROME

1. Pauline R. Clance and Suzanne A. Imes, "The Impostor Phenomenon in High Achieving Women: Dynamics and Therapeutic Intervention," *Psychotherapy: Theory, Research & Practice* 15, no. 3 (1978): 241–47.

2. Sandeep Ravindran, "Feeling Like a Fraud: The Imposter Phenomenon in Science Writing," The Open Notebook, November 15, 2016, www.theopennotebook.com/2016/11/15/feeling-like-a-fraud-the-impostor-phenomenon-in-science-writing/.

3. J. Sakulku and J. Alexander, "The Imposter Phenomenon," *International Journal of Behavioral Science* 6, no. 1 (2011): 73–92.

9 THE INEQUITABLE LEADERSHIP LOAD

1. Campaign Zero, "Mapping Police Violence," updated April 30, 2022, https://mappingpoliceviolence.org/.

2. Latoya Hill and Samantha Artiga, "COVID-19 Cases and Deaths by Race/Ethnicity: Current Data and Changes over Time," Kaiser Family Foundation, February 22, 2022, www.kff.org/coronavirus-covid-19/issue-brief/covid-19-cases-and-deaths-by-race-ethnicity-current-data-and-changes-over-time/.

12 PACING TOWARD PURPOSE

1. Edward Segal, "Leaders and Employees Are Burning out at Record Rates," *Forbes*, February 17, 2021, www.forbes.com/sites/edwardsegal/2021/02/17/leaders-and-employees-are-burning-out-at-record-rates-new-survey/?sh=2be9a5a06499.

ACKNOWLEDGMENTS

My deepest gratitude goes to the leaders who committed their time, energy, and expertise to contribute to this book. Thank you for sharing your stories with me through surveys and interviews. I am in awe of all that you have accomplished and have contributed to your teams, organizations, and communities at large. May your leadership be noticed and celebrated.

To all who have played a role in my own leadership journey, whether as former colleagues, classmates, friends, and supporters, know that this book is a combination and culmination of the many lessons I've learned from you along the way. I wouldn't be the leader I am without you.

Thank you to Jessica Faust for instantly seeing the value and urgency of bringing *Untapped Leadership* onto bookshelves and thank you to Jake Bonar and the team at Prometheus for guiding that toward reality. Denise Madre, thank you for your poignant feedback on the early draft, really pushing this work to evolve with impact.

And finally, thank you to my husband, Shaun, an untapped yet relentless leader who wholeheartedly cheered me and this book on every step of the way.